W9-DHN-351

CIVILIZATION
AND
GROUP RELATIONSHIPS

RELIGION AND CIVILIZATION SERIES

CIVILIZATION
AND
GROUP RELATIONSHIPS

A series of addresses and discussions

EDITED BY

R. M. MacIver

KENNIKAT PRESS, INC./PORT WASHINGTON, N. Y.

THE INSTITUTE FOR RELIGIOUS AND SOCIAL STUDIES
CIVILIZATION AND GROUP RELATIONSHIPS

Reissued 1969 by Kennikat Press
By arrangement with Harper & Row, Publishers, Incorporated

Library of Congress Catalog Card No: 68-26193
Manufactured in the United States of America

ESSAY AND GENERAL LITERATURE INDEX REPRINT SERIES

TO

Arthur Hays

AND

Iphigene Ochs Sulzberger

Who through
their personal and public lives
are creating better understanding
between men.

The authors contributing to this volume were invited to address the Institute for Religious Studies, because of the special contribution each could make to knowledge of the subject. Each chapter represents solely the individual opinion of the author. Neither the Institute nor the editors assume responsibility for the views expressed.

The Institute for Religious Studies, a graduate school conducted with the cooperation of Catholic, Jewish, and Protestant scholars, was established at the Jewish Theological Seminary of America through a gift from the late Lucius N. Littauer.

PREFACE

The Institute for Religious Studies has been carrying forward in various ways its deep interest in the challenge to unity and brotherhood raised by the prejudice and discrimination that separate group from group. This volume contains the addresses delivered in the second course devoted to the subject under its auspices. They are presented in their original form, so that the directness and appeal of the spoken word may as far as possible be conveyed to the reader.

We are concerned here not with the particular problem of any one group but with the problem of America, or rather with a world-wide problem that has a peculiar meaning for our democracy and is becoming continually more insistent among us. The leaders in every field of thought and of action are acutely aware of its magnitude and of its urgency. In this volume a number of them throw light on it from various angles, each approaching it from the viewpoint of his special competence.

Mr. Llewellyn goes to the roots of social behavior and shows how the "we-group" breeds exclusiveness against the "they-group," losing the greater community that would liberate and enrich their lives. Mr. Lindeman directs himself to the ramifying functional groups that lift themselves above the sense of the common and thus create tensions between group and group. Mr. Roucek fully illustrates his thesis that group discrimination is the background of the present war and the foreground of our dissensions at home. Mr. Brunner reveals the cost of our failure to realize in our educational systems the democratic concept of opportunity. Mr. Kandel advances the same lesson, bringing out the stratification of our youth that results from the inequality of opportunity. Mr. Lynd finds that our group discriminations have impaired "the grand affirmations of democracy," reducing them to negative prescriptions. Mr. Gifford sums up the social cost of being poor and points to the need of a further redistribution of wealth. Mr. Starr takes us into the labor unions and realistically deals with the grievous bars that deny to Negroes and other groups the opportunity to work. Bishop Tucker contributes the point of view of a man who understands the South, asking particularly how minorities should conduct themselves to aid in the process of their admission to full membership in the community. Father LaFarge deals with the role of myths in stimulating group tensions and with the role of religion in dispelling these myths. Finally, Mr. Young brings us squarely to the question of the specific means by which we may combat the evils of group discrimination and restore the democracy they imperil.

In this symposium there are differences of emphasis as well as differences of approach. But all our contributors agree on the vast threat that group discrimination makes against our unity and our well-being. In the light of these discussions we can certainly claim that the greatest peril of modern society is the exclusiveness of group against group, by means of which the stronger groups prevent the weaker from sharing the benefits and the opportunities of the community, by reason of which the stronger grow proud and intolerant and prejudiced, denying their common humanity, while the less advantaged grow bitter and frustrated. Thus on all sides rancor and cleavage increase, and the energies of men are turned from creativeness to destructiveness, from co-operative gain to universal loss. The consummation of this evil thing has been manifested to the world in Germany, the final destruction of community, the final inhumanity of man to man. But we are slow to take the lesson to ourselves. In spite of victory, what Mark Starr says remains true: "If group discrimination persists, Hitler wins and democracy is doomed."

There was a French philosopher and sociologist who wrote: "All I owe to you I owe to myself. What I do for you I do for myself. What I do against you I do against myself." These words, applying to groups as well as to men, contain the core of the lesson we should seek to learn.

The reader will observe that in this volume there is a strong consensus on the part social education can and should play in meeting the peril. It is true that we must attack on other fronts as well, particularly the economic. The antidiscrimination law recently passed in New York State is a fine achievement in that direction. But above all we must advance on the educational front. For the trouble roots in the indoctrinated attitudes of group to group. It is of primary importance to reform our modes of education everywhere to this end, and not only in the school but also in the home and in the church and in the exclusive club. We need a great continuous campaign against the forces of darkness. We have never tried it. We need to win another and even harder victory, a victory of the mind and not of the sword. For this fight we have never formed our ranks or marshalled our resources. It is a fight not only against group discrimination as such but a fight for truth against prejudice and misrepresentation, for the brotherhood of men, for the unity and strength of our land. To that fight this book is dedicated.

The Institute for Religious Studies desires to express its gratitude to those who have responded so generously to its invitation by preparing and delivering the addresses here given to the reader.

THE EDITOR

CONTENTS

I

THE NEED FOR A CHANGE OF ATTITUDE

BY

R. M. MacIVER, Ph.D.

Professor of Political Philosophy and Sociology, Barnard College and Columbia University

Last year the Institute for Religious Studies under the guidance of Doctor Finkelstein inaugurated a course called "Group Relations and Group Antagonisms." That was a novelty. It was also an advance. The subject is one that is kept too much in the background; it is a subject that is very little studied, on which there are very few, if any, courses anywhere. And yet this subject is of vital importance to us. It is a subject of great concern to many countries today and it is a subject of peculiar concern to the United States. It is not going too far to say that the harmony, the unity, and even the peace of this country depend on our being able to deal rightly, decently, with this matter.

I say it is a matter of peculiar concern to our country. In other countries you have some minority and majority problems. Usually it is a question there of one or maybe two—two or three at most—minorities set over against a dominant group or majority. With us, it is a much more inclusive question. Our country is crisscrossed with group divisions, and it is not a question of one majority over against one or even two or three or four or five minorities.

If any of you doubt the range of this question and the need of facing it, I would refer you to the published record of our last year's addresses in this course.[1] In that symposium you will find a number

[1] *Group Relations and Group Antagonisms,* distributed for the Institute for Religious Studies by Harper, 1944.

of samples of the kind of thing that is troubling our social life, simply some examples out of many, but enough to reveal to you or to anyone the nature and the extent of this problem.

We are a democracy, but in this respect we are offending against it all the time. The central conception of democracy, that which gives it its vitality underneath, is the conception that it is the person as person that counts; the person not as property owner, not as the member of any class, not as the child of wealth or prestige, not as belonging to this or that race or group or religion, but the person as person; the conception that as a person he should be given equal rights and equal opportunities with others, and that these various distinctions are from this point of view irrelevant.

It is for this conception that America stands before the world. It is a conception peculiarly associated with America, and right now we claim to be fighting to help to vindicate it against its bitter enemies.

And yet everywhere we find substantial discriminations, substantial contradictions of this idea and ideal of democracy. Everywhere throughout the country we find cleavages and divisions based upon differences that are essentially irrelevant to our common citizenship. Some of these discriminations are glaring and cry to heaven, particularly that against the Negro. Some of them are peculiarly offensive and most manifestly unjust, particularly the manner in which the Chinese group in this country has been and is being treated. Some of them are at this time ominous, particularly the growth of anti-Semitism. These are simply outstanding examples of a much more widespread evil, of a more general failure in our social life.

There is not an ethnic group in this country that somewhere is not disparaged, somewhere does not suffer some discrimination apart altogether from the question of worth or personality, some kind of frustration or some kind of repression. And therein is a denial—and it has tended to grow rather than to diminish—of the peculiar promise and the peculiar creed of America.

Take a coin out of your pocket and look at it. What do you see? *E Pluribus Unum,* one out of many, one built out of many, one nation born of many—of many what? Of many groups, tongues, religions, races. That is the claim and that is the promise of America, one nation made of many, accepting the differences, the contributions of all; joined, as Americans, in a unity that transcends the prejudices that divide people from people and group from group and race from race. That is the promise.

There have been recently some signs that people are awakening to this issue. I venture to count this course, the fact that it has been established under these auspices, as one of these signs. But most people do not in the least realize yet its extent, and they do not realize that it has been accentuated rather than lessened in recent times. Here is the justification for this course, if any were needed.

In this course we have brought together a series of competent authorities on various aspects of this whole problem. They will tell us, taking one aspect after another, how it manifests itself. They will tell us how it permeates into this or that area of our social life, how it distorts our social relationships, and they will also bring us suggestions for dealing with it. It is on that last question, the question of how we should approach the whole problem, that I want to say a few words to you now by way of introduction to those more specific talks.

It is one problem with many shapes, and while there are particular needs and particular aspects that require particular measures, yet, beyond that, since it is one problem, there is one broad solution to be found. In the last analysis, I believe it is a question of our re-educating ourselves, our people, all along the line, re-educating ourselves against group prejudices, which seep into us in subtle ways and ways that often we are quite unconscious of; re-educating ourselves so that we learn again what we have been tending to forget, the essentials of democratic living, the kind of living in which it is in the last resort the person who counts.

Above all, in order to meet this problem, we need a change of attitude. It is not the differences between men, not the differences between groups or races, that create this problem. It is our *attitude* toward those differences. What we need to do is to broaden and to enlighten our attitudes.

My predecessor at Columbia was Professor Giddings, and he was famous—if anybody knew anything about him they knew this thing about him—for the use of one expression that has entered into the language. He was always talking about "consciousness of kind." He was always saying that the thing that kept a society together was what he called "consciousness of kind."

That is all very well. The point is, however, that we have to redefine to ourselves, recomprehend what we mean by "kind." Who is our kind? Our kind means our kin. Who is my brother? Who belongs? Who is a citizen? We have to extend this concept of the consciousness of kind so that it will have meaning for a country like our own.

It is the unenlightened attitude toward difference, the prejudice evoked by difference, that is cramping in every respect our social life, that is limiting our horizon so that we cannot see people as people, we cannot see our fellow men, we cannot understand our relations to them, being blinded by these prejudices. We do not understand the needs of other groups, or the contributions that they bring, because we do not think of these groups except in terms of some preconceived prejudiced image.

It has been said that counsel is darkened by words without knowledge. Yes, but counsel is also darkened by knowledge without understanding, and a good deal of the darkening of counsel on this subject comes from those who give us facts, but facts without understanding.

I could quote instances, even among my own brethren—I mean people who are in some university position. I am thinking particularly of one anthropologist who is constantly perverting the notion of race, because he gives us facts and statistics in plenty, but without understanding. There are books crammed with figures and reeking with prejudice at the same time—though I shall not mention them here.

I want to give you instead an example of how facts without understanding, so far from enlightening us, are confirming our prejudices; whereas, the same facts with understanding would be more useful than anything else for the removal of these same prejudices.

We happen to have much statistics about crime. The statistical knowledge we have in this field is very much abused at times. For example, the records show that different ethnic groups, different racial groups, and so on, have different crime rates. There is more criminality shown by one group than another. Thus, if you take the crime rates of Negroes and whites, you will find that the crime rates of Negroes are much higher. In fact, the statistics look very bad for the Negro.[2]

I am going to give you some figures. I am going to give you here the arrests throughout the country for the last five-year period which we can quote, 1933 to 1938. The figures are given as so many out of each hundred thousand of the group concerned; 100,000 whites, 100,000 Negroes.

If you take 100,000 white males in the United States, you find that the arrests were 4,716 out of that 100,000. If you take the figures for female whites, out of 100,000, you will find the number is 416. Now turn to the Negroes, and you will find that the corresponding figure for the male Negroes is 14,332. For the female Negro it is nearly 3,800.

Let us follow this example a little further. The number of arrests is not the best indication, because, as every student knows, various things affect the number of arrests under different conditions. So let us take instead of arrests commitments to prison.

I should say first that the figures I have given you are taken from the Chicago area, because in the New York area the statistics do not distinguish between Negro and white. The figures I now go on to give are federal figures for the whole country.

You will find that with respect to commitments to prison the figures for Negroes exceed everywhere and often exceed many times the figures for whites. In fact, there is only one crime, as far as I could find looking down the list, in which the number of commitments to prison of Negroes was smaller than that of whites, and that was embezzlement! Can you guess why that should be so?

However, I want to give you the very worst figures. First, I will begin with homicide, which is the worst, or nearly the worst, of all.

[2] For the statistical evidence I am indebted to the article by Hans von Hentig, "The Criminality of the Colored Woman," University of Colorado Studies, Series C, Vol. I, No. 3, May, 1942.

To limit our story, and with all necessary apologies, I am going to take only the figures for the female population of the country. For native white females the figures are 2.8 commitments to prison for every million over 15 years of age in that population. For the Negro females, the corresponding figure is 46.4.

If you turn to larceny, you find that the commitments of native white females is 5.9—that is, per million native white females over 15 years of age in that population; whereas for Negro females the commitments are 38.1.

Lastly, I am going to take aggravated assault, and here the figures are: For the native white female, 0.8 per million of population, and for the Negro female, 21.8. There you are!

Figures don't lie. These figures aren't lying. In consequence, the believers in race discrimination get rather triumphant. Do not the figures show that a Negro is five or ten or twenty times as criminal with respect to these particular crimes as are the whites? What more do you want? Figures don't lie, but we can lie with the figures. That is what we do.

No criminologist—and I hope no sociologist—would draw any such conclusion from these figures as the believer in race discrimination draws, because what the criminologist does, and what we of course want to do, is to understand, to ask what these figures mean. When you do that, when you ask what they mean, the whole picture changes.

We know that where you have certain social conditions you always have a higher crime rate. For example, wherever you have a population with a very considerable sex disparity, that is, where there is a great preponderance either of males over females or of females over males, you have a higher crime rate. Incidentally, these things are not difficult to understand once you begin to examine them, but I haven't time to do that now.

Again, it is known to all students of the subject that wherever you have a high degree of illiteracy in a population otherwise literate, that group always shows a much higher crime rate.

Thirdly, we know again that wherever you have a group that suffers any marked economic discrimination, that group shows a higher crime rate; furthermore, wherever you have a group that is maintained at a lower economic level than the rest, surrounded by others at a higher level, that group shows a still higher crime rate.

Instead of making the comparison in terms of Negroes and whites, let us make it in terms of illiterates *versus* literates; or let us set the figures for people at one economic standard against those at another economic standard. As soon as we do that, the whole interpretation changes, the real meaning begins to appear.

If, in the language of the statistician, you standardize in terms of such things as illiteracy, economic level, sex disparity, and so forth, then you find that the rate for Negroes isn't higher on the average than the rate for whites.

There is the rate for illiteracy, for example. If you take one million illiterates, you will find that the rate for one million illiterates is about the same as the rate for one million Negroes. You have to take account of such factors to get the correct picture. And you will find that all four of the factors I have mentioned markedly distinguish the Negro group from the white. In the North there is a very great sex disparity; in the South there is a very great deal of illiteracy. Everywhere there is a great deal of economic discrimination and everywhere there is a tendency to a lower economic level.

White men under the same disabilities as the Negroes exhibit similar crime ratios. The ratios are the clearest indication of differences arising out of differential social conditions, and wherever you have those differential social conditions, you have the same phenomena. So you see how illicit it is to say, "Oh, it is because they are Negroes that you have this high rate," not taking into account that we have thousands of corroborations to show that where we have similar social conditions we have similar rates.

You see how the picture changes. You see what has happened to our original conception, our first image that there is something about the Negroes that tends to make them commit more crimes. And yet people take these crude figures—as the statistician calls them—and use them as appeals to prejudice, as appeals to group pride. They are glad to have these figures to confirm their prejudices. Nothing gives such a glow of righteousness to the prejudiced man as to find figures to confirm his prejudices; there they are, and, naturally, he doesn't want to go any further and ask about them.

These figures and similar so-called evidences have been taken all the time by interested groups, by those who for the sake of group egoism or for economic interest are fighting against our democracy. They are fighting to establish discriminations, and at the same time they are really fighting against the truth, which they refuse or do not wish to understand. They are fighting against our harmony and our peace; they are fighting against America.

Examples of this prejudiced use of evidence are all around us, and I could spend time, except that it is too late, in giving you many more. There is no group that is immune from this prejudice. I happen to belong to a university. My group is not immune from it. I don't suppose even church groups are immune from it. I know that other groups, labor groups, for example, are not immune from it. Group egoisms and economic interests are at work everywhere, and that is why it is important that we should bring these things out into the light.

So I come back to my starting point. What we need is a widespread re-education of our attitudes by a study of the social realities, confirming knowledge with understanding. The more we seek to understand our society, the more we shall see how baseless these prejudices are. The more we learn about the facts, seeking to find their meaning, the more we shall see that they lead us from this imputation to groups of peculiar inferiorities or peculiar vices, lead us to see that the real source lies in the differences that society creates for these groups. By seeing these things we shall be on the way to that improvement of our attitudes, that enlightenment of our attitudes, which is so important for us at this time. If there were only a way in which these things could be brought before multitudes of people! I don't know how it can be done, but I do hope that our group here will be a nucleus working in that direction.

II

GROUP PREJUDICE AND SOCIAL EDUCATION

BY

KARL N. LLEWELLYN, J.D.

Associate Professor of Law, Columbia University

One puffs up the importance of whatever problem he happens to be concerned with. The deeper you get into any problem of this complex world, the wider grows the range in which you discover your problem to be vital, and then tend to see it as exclusively vital. And the more you pack your mind with such implications, the less chance is left for sound perspective. Thus, for example, the whole world comes easily enough to shape up almost purely in terms of possible exhaustion of natural resources, or in terms of improvement or debasement of the human stock; or in terms of decay or recapture of spiritual values, or of the lag between man's powers to exploit natural forces and man's ability to control the uses to which the exploitation is put. Indeed, I think I could make a pretty powerful case for the limited span of human attention as being the focal problem of our world, to which one could with some persuasiveness reduce such matters as ignorance, waste, political apathy, threat to all long-range spiritual values, the lopsidedness of our thinkers, and even group prejudice.

In any event it is clear that both you and I must be on our guard against getting the present camera so close to the objective that one tremendous foot will obscure both the man and the landscape. Despite that, I shall urge that the problem of group prejudice comes as close to being a key problem of the modern world as any problem you can find; that it is for the foreseeable future a permanent problem; and what I may loosely call education is for that foreseeable future the only available line of palliative or solution. But by "education" I mean not merely formal education in schools nor the general initial rearing of the child; I mean the whole learning process that goes on as long as man is alive to learn. I mean, in a word, that there are ways of diminishing or conquering group prejudice, and that those ways can be put to work on adults as on children. They are hard and they are slow, but they are workable and they are good. And the way to begin is to begin.

The heart of what I have to say sums up thus: the country first, and then the world, face problems of effective and intelligent organization and reorganization on an ever-widening scale. Organization forced and controlled either merely from the top or by any single group among us will in your view and mine pollute the very springs of significant human living.[1] But grass-roots organization raises problems of producing enough mutual understanding to keep faction feeling from dwarfing all sense of the whole, enough mutual understanding to get the urges of our leadership as of our citizenry into something of an automatic balance. And to keep those urges so balanced, I shall try to show that group prejudice is the most fundamental handicap or obstacle or trap along that road. I shall try to

[1] This is not nearly as clear in fact as you and I tend to think it is. Very real values came eventually out of a unification of France which rested on ruthless suppression by the cruder North, first of an Albigensian and then of a Huguenot civilization curiously similar to ours, and, in between, of a Burgundy which I at least greatly admire. The Normans in England moved in a manner and with an organizing power and "racial" vigor that reads amazingly like a modern Nazi invasion, save only that they found the conquered land, to their surprise, becoming their "heartland." The Romans, on the other hand, whose long-range efforts we seem today to approve, drained their conquered territories in the "best" modern Nazi style and employed a thoroughness in subjugation penalties which the Nazis have not yet dared to match (December, 1943).

These matters deserve more thought than most of us give them. But I do not think that they have any business to affect our attitudes, our emotions, or our fighting convictions. There is only one sound reason even to begin to submit to a hypothetical future "verdict of history" about the nonworkability of a way of life one holds precious. That reason appears only if, after throwing all you have into the fight, you have been crushed flat. "Verdicts of history," even when they happen to prove "favorable," take a few hundreds of bitter years to get themselves rendered.

What we can do, however, is to observe that when organization is called for, it *is* called for, and to observe that *grass-roots* organization does not just happen; it calls both for grass roots and for machinery and for long, persistent upkeep effort on the machinery. For a fine example see Lilienthal, *TVA—Democracy on the March* (1944).

show also that we misconceive group prejudice when we think of it as primarily a prejudice *against* some one or more particular groups: as anti-Semitism, anti-Catholicism, anti-Anything-in-particular. It is instead at bottom a prejudice *in favor* of "My Own Group" as against *all* others, "pro-us" prejudice eternal, live, and waiting, ready to be focused and intensified against *Any* Other Group. And this makes things look very different, once you see it. For I shall try to show that our very ways of growing up produce this basis and drive for overwhelming group prejudices in all directions, and that our ways of living on as adults reinforce those prejudices at every turn. I shall therefore argue that corrective machinery must, if it is to be *effective,* operate on a mass scale, a truly people-wide scale, as contrasted with the de-prejudicing of any few and favored individuals. I shall argue that such meetings as this are drop-in-the-bucket stuff, if they just happen and pass, and that they are at their very best only drop-out-of-the-oilcan stuff—useful as a drop or three of oil can be useful or even indispensable in a squeaking joint, but doomed to be temporary and very minor palliatives unless and until we can get down to causes and to cures which both reach to the root and go to the mass. And because I find only short-range value either in merely viewing with alarm or in merely crying out for change of heart, I shall proceed (so far as I have been able to get) to speak of concrete measures of relief and cure. The measures will have four characteristics: First, they will be measures which promise, so far as employed, to work. Second, they will be measures which are capable of employment in our here and now, and with means and personnel which are at hand. Third, they will be measures which can be put to work in the little as well as in the large; which do not depend on any preliminary wide-scale political or social reform; which open for immediate work by individuals or by smaller groups as well as by a nation. Lastly, they will be measures already sufficiently under way to be making real dents on the problem; though only dents.

Let me clear up one point, however, before going further. This discussion is going to be one of conditions as we find them, whether or not we like what we find. It will therefore be an unpleasing discussion, because in this matter conditions are unpleasing in the extreme. It is going to be a discussion not of ideals and good things, but of hard-headed and hard-eyed means and measures to deal with continuing conditions which in spots are not only hard and tough but also nasty. I happen to be a realist in jurisprudence, in sociology, and in psychology, and the job of a realist is to begin by seeing exactly what he is up against and by striving never to let what he wants and hopes for and will fight for get in the way of spotting what he is up against. The second job of a realist is to find ways and means that will *work*, in moving toward where he wants to go: to implement ideals with hands and feet that stand on and can take hold of the here and now. Now there is abroad in the land a silly and false line of thinking—or better, of nonthinking—which proceeds on a queer assumption that such hard-eyed study of ways and means, of hands and feet and machinery, betokens or even proves a lack of interest in ideals and right goals. It is a line of nonthinking which rests on an assumption that all right answers are *single,* so that to answer "Yes" to anything is of necessity to answer "No" to anything else. Thus it is the same line of nonthinking which leads to such conclusions as that "we must win, simply because we are right" or that it is enough, generally, in this world of ours to behave rightly and feel rightly. Whereas the whole course of human history indicates that while faith and ideals can sometimes win battles, faith and ideals alone cannot win wars; that while faith and ideals can move societies, they cannot, alone, *build* societies nor yet build up new generations within societies; that while it is death to be without them, yet they cannot, alone, continue life. They provide the breath and the blood and the spirit of life and society, but they provide neither the bony structure nor the muscle nor the nervous integration and balance nor yet the food and digestive machinery. And since I am speaking to people whose faith and ideals I can presuppose as definitely as I can presuppose my own, I shall, deliberately, insist throughout this lecture on the *What-Else-in-Addition* that is essential to make those ideals take on working reality.

The first point I want to make is that the basic process of "socializing" the newborn human animal is a process of "antisocializing" him at the same time. For a century ahead, at least, it seems to me that this has to continue so.[2]

Look it over. The fundamental fact is that the human being is a *group* product, and therefore develops into a group member, absorbing many vital aspects of his environing group.[3] The next fact is that this building of groups (like this building of the newborn into effective group membership and so into being a person instead of a cross between an angry wildcat and a haphazard cyclone) appears, as it just proceeds to happen, to be almost in equal measure a consolidating business and at the same time and by the same means an *excluding* business. I happen not to have noticed this much in the literature (except for Sumner), although it is too obvious not to have been remarked on many times.

It is in any event vital for our problem. Sumner—as so often—cut to the heart of it; man lives in an In-group; and to any In-group any and every other group is an Out-group. An In-group or We-group is indeed hard to conceive except by contrast to the Others who are not In, but are Out, not We, but They.

This has four different aspects, all vital to our problem.

The first is the fact and the utter necessity of channeling each new small ball of random energy into *group* ways before it (he or she) can become either at all bearable or recognizable as a "person." If you have not thought about this before, think about it now. It is quick to prove. In the matter of bearability, imagine a baby born with the physique of twenty-one years and meditate on a baby's horrible but now frustrated rage at weaning or being left alone or at colic or simple undiagnosed desire, plus the young child's pleasure in watching fire grow and in smashing anything that either resists or smashes with a noise. In the matter of recognizability as a person, consider speech

[2] Although I get glimmers of procedures, here and now politically impossible, which *could* produce an effective coalescence on a mass scale.

[3] *E.g.*, at ten, at six, even at three, the boy line of any tradition produces (in the mass) sharply different reactions and attitudes from the girl line; or the French or the Dutch from the American. Subdivide any of the suggested categories, so as to make more and more things "equal" and you will still get the suggested result: *e.g.*, American upper-income single-child boy *vs.* girl; French-Breton white agricultural *vs.* Wisconsin white agricultural, or either *vs.* Mississippi white share-cropper agricultural.

(which language differences show to be one of our sets of group-ways) and ask yourself whether you are prepared really to recognize as a "person" any human being with normal organs of hearing and speech who at twenty-one still babbles.

The second aspect is equally quick to see, and the matter of language offers the quickest way to see it. Not *human* group-ways, but the group-ways of *My Particular Group,* are what each budding "I" is slowly shaped to fit into *and so to demand of others.* The American child does not grow up speaking or expecting French. He plays "Farmer in the Dell," not *"Sur la pont d'Avignon."* He knows of Washington, Lincoln, Roosevelt, not of Charlemagne, Jeanne d'Arc, Pétain. His heart rises to the Stars and Stripes and is bothered when he has trouble with certain high notes in *Our* national anthem. If you see this, you must go on to see further: if he is being raised Back Bay, "The Irish" are different, threatening, and bad. If he is "Boston Irish," he looks with scorn upon a waning effort of civilization typified by Back Bay. Save in an utter crisis of the nation, "My" group is not, for most purposes, The People of these United States, it is for most and for deep purposes "The people I grew up among," and pretty narrow: *"Unsre Leit";* "White folks is white folks"; "Public School is so indiscriminate"; "the dirty Harps," "the lousy Orangemen."

The third aspect is this, and you will please take time enough to get it clear: Those ideal, ethical, social values which mean not only bearability of the person but forward drive, input of extra work, service, the quest for loveliness, that wonder by-product, nobility of soul—these are instilled and develop only out of In-group, out of We-group rearing and training. They are directed to, focused on, produced by "Us-ness." They are what Civilization most vitally needs. They represent its Soul. But for all except the inspired they grow out of, and so by the nature of that growth are most limited to, the In-group, the felt We-group. I speak of mass phenomena, of bulk occurrence, not of occasional transcendent individuals. I speak of voting power, within a political democracy, of the many who, if a leader gets too far ahead, make him a "leader" without followers.[4] The raising, then, of the growing ego to have and respond to these "In-group," these "We-group" ways, attitudes, ideals—this is not only our necessity for keeping our society alive, but it is our hope for all that is worth while.

But the fourth aspect is what shocked men as Sumner underscored it. Man lives in an In-group, a We-group. The recognized and cherished virtues in social contacts apply with full effect to all other members of that We-group: loyalty, honesty, self-restraint, courtesy, support in need, self-sacrifice; as contrasted with concealment, deceit, overbearingness, contempt, disregard, robbery, killing—which are in savage societies the normal and proper ways of dealing with members of *any* They-group. Take the last first: in our own society the righteous and laudable killing of "Out-group" or "They-group" members is limited to war and the general war area of thought (*e.g.* the spy about to get away with military secrets). But it needs only that you note our celebration of aviation aces or of enemy casualties in general to make clear that we—like all other men but prophets—still run our ways, our morals, our ideals, on two different levels which divide flatly according to We-ness and to They-ness. The things you need to see if you have not yet thought about them are these: (1) that you can sympathize to the heart with deceit and killing ("successful ambush") when directed against a They-group

[4] My reading shows no leadership toward One-ness that compares in immediate effectiveness with that of Moslemism in its earlier conquests. Certainly, in part, because the choice was simple: Confess belief or die. Certainly, in part, because the mechanism of "confessing belief" was equally simple: one short formula. But beyond both of these lay a power, not as yet analyzed to my knowledge, of producing in the conquerors, despite differences in language and other vitally recognizable ways, a seemingly unparalleled feeling of "We-ness" with those who had confessed belief. My very insufficient reading on the point suggests a degree of acceptation of the conquered which as against any comparable case would be as "sociologically impossible" as is the modern student-run Law Review of these United States: a scientific periodical matching in quality the best professional journals of the law or of any other discipline, responsibly edited by men who are still ungraduated, unadmitted students, with decision-making staffs turning over every year, with no editorial personnel in office or training for more than a rough two years, and with entrance on such training preceded by a bare year's study in the discipline. I have managed finally to explain this last "sociological impossibility"; the results persuade me that no line of inquiry is more fruitful than inquiry into such impossibilities.

and any of its impersonal individual members (contrast: one single hunted escaper from a prison camp, hungry, weary, just inside your door with the hounds approaching); (2) that deceit, robbery and killing apart, you have They-group attitudes toward a considerable number of "they's" within these United States. If you practice law, how long since you have been willing to hire a woman as a law-clerk? If you own a house, what do you think of having a colored family "buy in" next door? If you are a union man, what is your attitude toward "rugged individualists" on the neighboring machine? If you are a Republican, how do you feel about a New Dealer? If not robbery, bold fraud, killing (which we in our civilization reserve for They-groups at *war* with us), at least we indulge, within our own America, the other ancient attitudes toward our They-groups: distrust, disgust or ridicule, fear, hate, checked in minor part but only in minor part by religion, morals, manners, and the compulsion of the law. I challenge you who listen. Do you dare claim your souls are clean, in this? No snobberies, disgusts, fears, or hates where you feel yourselves (not personally, but as *group* members) at an advantage? No inverse snobberies, resentments, fears, or hates where you feel yourselves (not personally, but as *group* members) discarded?

These are the facts of life in this matter, as they result. But to see our problem, we must go on into *how* they result. And that goes back to an eternal phenomenon: the newborn infant.

An In-group, a We-group, is the only machinery known to us, I repeat, for producing out of each small groping squaller that something different which we can recognize as a *person*. The psychologists tell us of certain needs for "security" in the growing human being; and it appears to be "family," or persons who are family members known *and designated as such* ("father," "mother," "brother," "uncle," "nurse"), who first satisfy and reinforce and then symbolize that security. You must really see this, and feel it. You see it when any man stranger is hailed by a lisper as "Dad-dy" and approached accordingly. It is a queer man stranger who does not respond. You see it at a later age when a dinner guest is introduced as "Mr. Struthers" and therefore let alone unless he makes advances, whereas if he is introduced as *"Uncle* Jack" he is promptly climbed on and has his hair pulled (and knows he has to take it). He has been labeled, *pro hac vice* he has been made a We-group member. This carries over throughout life. If you want "the govamunt" (which too commonly spells milch cow or sloppy waste) or "the burocracy" (which spells blindness, tyranny, or red tape) to appear live, close, warm, strong, a right subject for affection, respect, and pride—then you speak of "Uncle Sam."

But at the same time you see that even so early and by this mechanism, the We-group circle demonstrates its closing; inward, and also outward. There are freedoms of behavior within, there is a tightening up of teamwork as against the outside, from "company manners" on through to "not washing dirty linen in public." There is the building up of loyalties, tolerances, ways of adjustment, the recognition of "Our" ways, "Our" standards, "Our" rightnesses, to which the budding "I" must shape himself, and does. What I want to suggest is only that the concept of "We" as it is thus in fact created in the child is at the same time and by the same almost-necessity a concept of "They" as being persons to whom the same duties, the same sympathies, are *not* owing, and *as against* whom the "We's" line up together—as of course. The child as he becomes a *person* acquires, by the very process of becoming one, these two ingrained and contradictory sets of attitudes, patterns of action, emotion, and thought. The "We" set is the set on the growth of which both the child and his civilization utterly depend. But to build that set he *has* to build also that "They" set which threatens to disrupt both him and his civilization, and which applies to anyone who is not part of his "Us."

Now I do believe it to be humanly possible to rear individual children with an almost indefinitely expansible set of "We" attitudes, and with no sharp crystallization of these socially disruptive "They" attitudes. But there is no *large*-scale rearing of this type that now goes on. The current multitude of "names" of scorn and insult "upward" or "downward" or "crosswise" are enough both to witness and focus the contrary: "Sissy," "Lilyfinger," "Mick," "Kike," "Nigger," "Spic," "Hunyak," "Wop," "White Trash," "Damnyankee." Or consider the high tolerance and unity that find expression in "the effete East," "the sticks," "rube," "city slicker," "agitator," "goon," "white collar." Whether by section, by national or race origin, by occupation, by financial or social position, by residence with reference to the railroad tracks, the labels are there to gather, there to spread, there to intensify "They" attitudes. The labels have, also at times, a terrifying indiscriminate over-breadth: consider, today, with the Chinese as our allies, and the overwhelming Philippine majority on Bataan, "yellow bastard." And they are group labels, impersonal, to stick as labels on any person, and make him thus cease to seem wholly a person. To us, as to the savage, "man," "full man," "real person," means "one of us."

All of this could in itself be relatively harmless; it could in itself conduce even to a fuller and more enjoyable life; but only on one condition. That condition is that the wider Unity shall be so powerfully felt, perceived, and acted on that the great *Team* with its team play and team membership definitely dominates all factions and all faction feelings. Within a felt dominant Unity you can call names, curse, and seem to scorn, because the felt unity talks more deeply than your words. Within a sufficiently felt unity, felt differences can produce more of affection than of irritation. Again the family shows the picture. If it is a family instead of a failure, it remains a team. That even the family becomes so often a failure instead of a family gives us a first indication of the power of the *divisive* drives which rise in our culture from the very shaping of the child into a person.

Now it is in my mind, with no particular desire to glorify any nonexistent rosy past, that this particular problem of group prejudices —this problem first of the outbalancing of "We" attitudes by "They" attitudes and, second, of their too great outbalancing—that this problem was not so severe before our nation was industrialized. I do find nastily divisive currents, say, in our earlier nineteenth century. The Sections were forming up, the States then showed an isolationism greater than today's; the social and political bitterness of the "safe" men against Jackson's "rabble" makes today's anti-Rooseveltism seem thin as dishwater; the Know-Nothings do not present a pretty picture; nor are melted tar and knife-edged fence rails gentle instruments. Yet, looking all that fairly in the face, I cannot find it so distressing as the picture of today. And the reason is clear. The reason is that the mere growing up in a community of 1830 or 1840 gave you, whether you wanted it or not, *some* view and *some* understanding of a *Whole* of which you were a part and of that Whole as something to which you owed a real responsibility. Then factional battles were as bitter and often as dirty and cruel as a family blowup; but even when drowned in interest, hate, and physical or emotional drunkenness, they were yet carried on over a heavy undertone of the *felt team* that still consisted of the *Whole*. I have never been sure of this, and study of Civil War times, both North and South, has made me less sure; it *may* be only that the divisive forces were still, one by one, too little organized, too small in size and gathered strength to tear things utterly apart, no matter how far each part had lost sense for the Whole. Nonetheless, I still think I describe accurately.

What bothers me today is that today I see no as yet adequate machinery at work in civil life and on the mass scale for leavening our "They-group" attitudes with this needed underlying feel and consciousness of Total Team, while the They-group attitudes apply to all who do not happen, by training, to be strictly "We," and today that means for each of us to an ever-widening major fraction of the population.

For observe first that merely growing up, today, has no need to produce any understanding at all—except in national crisis—along the line of the great team. In the country, certainly in a one-crop area, there is little but lopsidedness to be had: the whole industrial or financial phase of the world is "They." In a city big enough to have high-school districts, the situation is worse, because "They" are not only present but "They" are close at hand, for active, personalized enmities to develop, while the whole, even of the city itself, it is far too big for a youngster to fathom by mere growing up. The best long-tested American institution to meet this, and it is both peculiarly American and a social invention of amazing power, is the single high school of the smaller Mid-Western town or city. I am not touting such a high school as a wholly "democratic" institution, nor as perfection. I am fully aware, for instance, that the Negro (or the Mexican) gets little comfort from it. I know, even at its best, the overdominance of those better situated economically and the snobberies and heartburnings which result. But I trust I am enough of a sociologist to recognize in snobbery (which I abominate) probably the most potent single force for self-improvement in a mobile society. And I state categorically that the nearest working approach thus far offered on a wide scale in our civilian life to the fabled melting pot is found in just these high schools. The *bulk,* the overwhelming bulk, of the kids comes out of them with some real living feeling of a Total Whole, and with some real *approach* to living "We-group" attitudes that have bridged, for instance, the railroad tracks and a fair portion of the religious, economic, racial, and political gulfs within the community.

The sociological processes involved in furthering or breaking down group prejudice are relatively simple to see and to describe, and it is very queer that they have received so little attention. I am not referring to "processes" of the large, loose sort called "accommodation," "co-operation," etc. I am referring to the detailed daily mechanisms by which individual persons, in types of situation which occur and recur as recognizable types, proceed to react with some mass reckonability.

The first point is that the We-attitudes are almost always expansible to a material degree, and that when their scope is expanded to include new persons it tends strongly to be so expanded *en bloc.* The new person is *accepted.* If a child receives Mr. Struthers as "Uncle Jack," he takes the new uncle utterly. When you discover your outsider to be "just like one of us," you "take him in." Note the processes of thought and feeling. You adopt him *into* your We-group. Without greatly thinking about it, you thereby in your own feeling *divorce* him from his old group. You also feel that you have been very generous and that he owes both equivalent gratitude and an obligation to react wholly like "one of us." Here lies danger; as danger lies also in your sudden shift from trial acceptance or acceptance with reservations, conscious or unconscious, into real acceptance.[5] But the process is a widener of understanding and of the range of feeling. One perceives that *some* "real people" can grow elsewhere.

But the second point is that such expansion tends strongly to be limited to the particular person concerned. As a mass phenomenon it depends first of all on *recurrent* and *close* contacts with that person, an "otherwise" acceptable individual. But to get beyond the phase of taking in just him (and of *pro tanto* seeking to take him out of his "own" group), to move into an attitude of wider openness to and understanding of They-groups in general, there must be in the picture also some *grouping* which can be seen and felt as a wider We-group of which both acceptor and acceptee bcome a part. That is just what the single local high school offers, and over a four-year period. In primitive life the newcomer is adopted into the family or the tribe—he is drawn wholly in, and wholly out of his old group. In our society both or more of those concerned can become members of a We-group different from their old We-groupings: they can marry and form a *new* family; they can enter the high school; they can become active both in "the party" and in the same party "club."

The third point has to do with certain vital attitudes toward evidence and occurrences and troubles. The We-attitude is one of sympathy and indulgence toward the individual concerned, and it is that of reading all evidence fast and firmly to the glory of Our group. The They-attitude is one of suspicion and condemnation of the individual in question, and it is that of reading all evidence fast and firmly to the discredit of His group. Bad taste, evil intent, dirty dealing, crime, are alleged of an individual, or some happening suggests them. If he is of your We-group you "cannot believe it of him," "there must be some mistake," " 'We' aren't like that"; at the worst, he is utterly nontypical of Us, thank God. But if he is of one of your They-groups you take the report at once, at face, and on its worst interpretation; "There, you see: that's just the way 'They' are"; the

[5] This has its dangers of throwback, precisely because it obscures the need for detailed adjustment to and working out of the remaining powerful divergences. Complete acceptance sets up expectations of complete fitting in; and disappointed expectations kick back with peculiar violence. The phenomenon is most strikingly observable in cross-group boy-and-girl relations before and after marriage.

worst at once displays to you the essential character of Them All. It is the good which is exceptional, as to Them. The likable and fine is therefore read exactly in reverse. The best that *any* of Us does is *typical* of Us; we swell with pride. The unmistakably fine on the part of one or three or forty of Them, seen from the outside, leads only to a grudging recognition that there *are* exceptions—if the report is true.

Now these destructive They-ways of interpretation—these ways of reading and using that new experience which is the adult's line of ongoing education—these ways intensify in the measure in which there exist well-integrated particular patterns of adverse, scornful, fearful, or hateful concept about the nature of any particular They-group concerned—"Capital" and "the Bosses" or "Labor" and the "Unions"; "Bourbons" or "Communists"; "Jews," "Catholics," "Babbitts," "Bible-Belters," "Long-Haired Professors," or Big Endians and Little Endians of any other label. And the devastating effect of such They-ways of reading each particular incident piles up in terms of the multitude of incidents which come to superficial notice, devoid of any healthy backlog of contact at first hand with an adequate number of persons of the particular They-category; devoid of any healthy backlog of *recurrent* discovery that the sloganized "They" pictures handed down within the We-group prove with some regularity when tested in action and actual contact to be distorted calumnies. One recalls Lincoln Steffens' amazement and distress as the political bosses against whom he was crusading turned out so regularly to be people—people who in so many ways plainly earned his admiration. Thus the rapid modern increase of "news," even apart from any deliberate distortion, becomes less a reducer than an increaser of any group prejudices which have become organized into integrated and current sloganized *whole*-patterns, a "conqueror of distance" in the physical sense which tends rather to increase "social" gulfs. (In contrast, some of the continuing radio programs develop contact enough with groups different from oneself to bridge gaps—if one listens regularly to such programs depicting one's They-groups; as do some of the comic strips, which I suspect get a much less selective audience.)

Put these three factors together: whole-hog acceptance, if any acceptance at all—removing the accepted individual from any persuasiveness regarding his still wholly unaccepted group. The dependence of acceptance on recurrent and favorable personal contact in the context of a felt group of which both the acceptee and the acceptor are a working part, and the relative rarity of those conditions. The set adverse and differential "type" interpretation of any surface or secondhand experience, and today's multiplication of such experience. These are the ongoing disruptive mechanisms or machineries, ever new because they are re-created in raising almost every child into the social virtues and with the social values which we need.

What can be set against them is this—slow, painful, but effective: (1) To run, in close and continued contacts, into not one or two, but into a series of persons from an Others- or They- or Out-group, and to begin to see them from inside a wider felt group-unity, this is materially to change one's They-attitude not only toward them as persons, but toward all further surface experience which concerns each of the particular Others-groups. (2) Moreover, since the basis of group prejudice is the We-group attitude as against all other groups, that basis is severely shaken by solid countering experience with even a single They-group. Such experience is not enough, for most. It can be bulkheaded off, and tends to be, leaving other "hates" or "fears" quite open still. But the second job on another They-group is thrice and more as easy as the first. (3) For a person to do this with members of a series of marked and known Others-groups breaks down those same attitudes toward *all* Others-groups, within a given limit. The limit varies with the person; but it is always vastly wider than the circle of the direct experience. Its radius is determined, so far as I can see, in the first instance, by the *felt* range of the greater Whole within which the Others-groups have, as they were met, been seen as included. Almost always that seeing has a series of peripheries, reaching outward with differential intensity and queer exclusive criteria. But the essential game is won with the first major and *general* breakdown of the Others-attitude.

What the high school mentioned above accomplishes is to get this done early in life, at least on the community scale, and commonly to get it done with regard to several different Others-groups at once; yet late enough in life so that it requires some conscious thought to digest the results—thought which goes some distance to drive them home.

One must, however, in the single high school and elsewhere, note one qualifying and danger-producing factor: close contact of members of different groups can, under unfavorable circumstances and absent highly skilled management, result in increased bitterness. Where the background is one of established ideology, especially where one group is on the rise and resentful, the other on the defensive and afraid, individuals are prone to meet not as people but as representatives, with loyalties and with closed fronts, and the contacts are likely to be those of war. That fact gives some color of reason—only, in my view, a color—to the attitude of the Army toward our colored citizens in this war. The reason why I think the choice made to be a mistaken choice is that the overwhelming tendency of any decent army is to work out group loyalties in terms of the "outfit," which transcends any type of group background of its members, so that mixing "unlikes" into "outfits" breaks down prejudice.

And that is why the Armed Services are providing today the most hopeful antiprejudice mass-scale operation we have ever seen. It has been skilfully done, the mixing of the population into the smaller units: continuous contact in a common setting of a new group-loyalty lived with, lived in, small enough to see and grasp and stir pride, yet an inescapable part also of a National Whole—with the members of different They-groups so many and so mixed that they cannot be felt and fought as mere "representatives." Here is a thing to give heart, and to set against the political dangers of a pressure group of twelve millions of veterans. It is doubly hopeful because it occurs among the young, who will be raising the next generation. While, at the moment of saying this, the heart bleeds to see a body of our people larger than the body drawn into the services still substantially cut off from the most effective prejudice-dissolving processes.

One must not, however, count too heavily upon the effects of armed service. Veterans return to a life organized along civilian lines; and how far Joe and Stan will then prove to have been cases of merely "personal" acceptance remains a problem. I count here, somewhat, on the Legion posts to do a thing our ordinary political clubs have done less well. In the latter it has been found useful, repeatedly, to lump the club around a group unity of another kind, largely Polish or Irish or whatever. The Legion's unity is of a cross-group kind, and can be more so, according to the way in which Posts come to be established.

I find hope, too, despite blindness and setbacks, in the labor field. I find a definite trend there in the direction of more understanding between managers and labor leaders, and in the direction of each group's undertaking some burden of "selling the other to its constituency." Leaders have leverage, and not only in lessening the enmity against "adversaries." You see what can be done when you see the skill with which the cafeteria workers in this city were brought to accept colored workers into the union and on the job: use of a time of labor shortage, use of Mrs. Roosevelt's entertainment of Marian Anderson, careful selection of the first colored workers to be hired for "front" work, flat head-on meeting of the first few cases of "either she goes or I go"—and the *unreasoning* barrier is down. There remains friction; but it is dwindling friction, and contact within the wider unity has come and continues.

But as one moves into his own small effort, in neighborhood or any other groups, along such lines, and in regard to building chances for contact, and then effective contacts, between any groups, it pays to remember that bites too large are fraught with indigestion. Group prejudice roots deep because it roots in infancy. It roots deep because it roots in the very origins of our finest loyalties and loves. It is tricky because of these things, and also because "acceptance" leads so lightly to overexpectation, and seems always to imply a debt on the part of the person accepted. Lurking for the occasion of sudden crisis or disappointment are all the nasty feelings and all the nasty labels: "So you're only a dirty ——, after all!" (Fill in to suit.)

An individual's own part begins slowly and continues long. You do some reading, detailed sympathetic studies made from inside some group that is strange and, preferably, a bit obnoxious to you. You do steady, heavy policing of your own reactions to incidents and hearsay about particular happenings, trying out the very troublesome job of weighing *fairly* what you read and hear—or half see. You discover that it is hard to see a person as a person, rather than as a member of a group, without resenting and reacting in resentment. You take on membership and work in at least one group in which you have a chance to move—*very* carefully—toward steady and satisfactory contacts between members of different and partly antagonistic groups, and you build by work more than by talk on the wider value and purpose that joins all; which means you must be choosing for your work a group that has a purpose worth having. It is all prosaic and humdrum and time-consuming and terribly slow. It is baffling because other people will not understand and will insist on doing the wrong things, or choosing the wrong times. It is uncomfortable because it really disturbs some of your own most comforting and well-laid prejudices; and nothing is so pleasant, so effort-saving, as such a prejudice. Yet I think this game, played over the years by each of us, is our necessary contribution to our citizenship. And I know it is fun, and a source of richer living. Some of us even get into a position of leverage and bring down suddenly a whole section of some wall of prejudice the others have been undermining through the years. But without that prior undermining no leader could bring it down—except as, on occasion, some shrewd heads and hands are in a key position at some actual or possible mixing bowl and shape not the people but the conditions of their meeting and their work—in terms not of Great Ideals alone (the Flag, the Nation, Brotherhood of Man) but of small daily jobs in face-to-face tangible outfits, too, so that the people reshape—educate—themselves into not only a new We-group, but a We-group built around a conscious job: that is, a Team.

III

GROUP TENSIONS IN AMERICAN SOCIETY

BY

EDUARD C. LINDEMAN, B.S.

Teacher and Extension Worker,
New York School of Social Work

Two remarkable statements were made to the American public a few weeks ago: one by the Speaker of the House of Representatives in Washington and the other by Charles Wilson, vice-chairman of the War Production Board. Both of these public officials chose the same topic, namely, the disunity now prevailing in American life. The former, Representative Rayburn, spoke with deep feeling to his colleagues in Congress and Mr. Wilson directed his warnings to the National Association of Manufacturers. What is chiefly remarkable about these public pronouncements is the fact that the disunity which they fear has arisen in the midst of the greatest war in which our nation has ever been involved. One might have expected disunity at the close of such a war but certainly not while the nation is struggling against formidable external enemies. Indeed, this manifestation has never occurred in our previous history, except on a minor scale during the war with Mexico in 1848. Hence the question becomes pertinent: if we cannot find national unity in the midst of a gigantic war, how will it be when the threat of the enemy is removed?

Because this question is important and is filled with portent I have chosen to discuss some of the causes of our present disunity, hoping of course, as all educators must, that an understanding of the causes will naturally lead to a search for remedies.

The common term now applied to our internal differences is "tension," a word which, like so many used in the social sciences, has been borrowed from the physical realm. The word "tension" has enjoyed a steady expansion in English: beginning with the notion of strain placed upon materials, it has now come to include the following meanings: muscular strain, a point of electrical discharge, the converse of pressure, mental strain, psychological anxiety or unrest, and finally (although so lively a word will probably continue to expand) social strain, or tension between the various groups which constitute society. It is interesting to note that one of the connotations which this word carries is that of a breaking-point, a violent eventuation, if the strains are not released or removed.

In ordinary times it may be assumed that certain group-to-group tensions are a sign of societal health. Their existence means that a wholesome form of striving for the realization of group interests is in process. When, however, such tensions multiply and *intensify* in time of war it must be assumed that the main direction of society has somehow gone wrong; speaking more particularly, when this phenomenon takes place in a democratic society such as ours, it may be assumed that the regular and accustomed processes of democracy are no longer functioning satisfactorily; that is, are not resolving the inner conflicts through methods of discussion and experiment. Already one hears prophecies concerning the coming Balkanization of the United States, a term which seems to imply regional, racial, religious, and political incompatibilities of so deep a character as to preclude a workable synthesis. Shortly after World War I Justice Charles E. Hughes warned us that our institutions, especially those designed to establish justice and sustain our liberties, might not be able to stand the strain of another great war, even though we should be on the victorious side. His warning should be taken into account by those who are now confronted with that war which he dreaded and that coming peace fraught with perils as great as those of war itself.

The analysis which follows is composed of unequal elements thrown together without any attempt at classification or weighting. In striving to bring some clarity of thought to bear upon the question, What accounts for our present group-to-group tensions and the consequent manifestation of national disunity? I am including factors that are antecedent to the War as well as those that are attendant upon the War.

1. In modern society all individuals who wish to "count" must belong to groups. There is more than irony in the remark that "an optimist is a person who thinks he can get somewhere without a pressure group." This feature of modern life we accept and it is not, indeed, inconsistent with democratic principles. A pressure group is an instrument of petition and our Constitution expressly provides for the petitioning act. No trouble can arise from the existence of multiple groups, so long as the ultimate ends for which these groups are striving constitute a coherent and self-consistent cluster of values. I do not say that this cluster should or can be permanent or even stable. A "grand view" or what Harold Laski calls "the great and common ends of life" cannot be expected to be of long endurance. Indeed, the grand view shines most brilliantly when a society is on the way toward self-discovery and self-announcement; it tends to dim whenever there arises a sense of having arrived. It seems to me fair to assume that one of the difficulties of the present moment attaches to the fact that our group aims do not now coalesce, they are not confluent with respect to ends to which all may in general subscribe.

An illustration may be taken from the bitter conflict now existing between organized farm groups and organized labor groups. The former seem to want inflation while the latter fear this same eventuality. But is it not basically true that the long-term interests of the two groups are complementary, not antithetical? Is it not true that the farmer's best prospect for a steady market lies in the possibility of increasing and stabilizing the incomes of urban industrial workers? Why, then, do these two groups travel in opposite directions? How does it happen that they have lost sight of their common ends? In this instance I take the common end to be security, prosperity, and a high standard of living for both groups. Is the existing state of tension between agricultural and industrial workers due to false leadership, inadequate leadership, faulty education, cultural diversities, political manipulations? If even partial answers were available for these queries, we could then begin a remedial program, and this analytical procedure seems to me to be required for each of our group-to-group tensions.

2. Modern functional groups (trade-unions, manufacturers' associations, chambers of commerce, farm organizations, professional associations, et cetera) have come to be gigantic superstructures which no longer rest upon the solid base of smaller friendship groupings. They undertake to be operational without being fraternal. This conception of social organization is an open invitation to selfish individualism concealed within collective shells. Hence, our mechanistic collectivism cannot lead to a unifying national purpose. To join such a collective unit is to choose an enemy but not to gain a friend. I sat recently at lunch with a group of workers in a huge war plant. They were all members of a trade-union, since they worked in a closed shop. It seems to me that I have never heard more bitter denunciation of trade-unionism than that which came from these men. I found no loyalty between these men as individuals nor between them and their union. I happen to believe in trade-unionism; in fact, I do not see how we can expect the proper functioning of democracy unless there are strong trade-unions striving to validate the workers' interests. But this strength must be a democratic strength. Equality and liberty are values which cannot stand alone: they are dependent upon fraternity. Democratic consequences cannot be anticipated otherwise.

What has been said above points toward new techniques of social organization and these apply, not merely to the functional groups included above but to all forms of human association, churches and educational institutions as well as trade-unions and chambers of commerce. Functional organization which lifts itself above friendship, neighborhood, and community may become a source of power, but it will be power capable of destroying democracy at its roots.

3. Tensions arise in a society at war for a variety of reasons. War, and particularly a total war such as the present one, demands a common sacrifice; this claim elicits a corresponding demand for common benefits, especially on behalf of hitherto disprivileged groups. War

creates an atmosphere in which aggressive impulses are esteemed as virtues; non-combatants, in whom these aggressive impulses are also distributed, are deprived of the opportunity to express their latent aggression, deprived, that is, of sharing in this wartime virtue; hence they find other channels and the most convenient outlet is furnished in already existing group rivalries. In wartime the folkways become more pliable. It thus happens that long-standing injustices which have become embedded in the folkways as accepted discriminations may now be more readily "broken." It is to be expected that depressed and disprivileged groups (economic groups, classes, racial groups, et cetera) will strive to enhance their status during a period of war. (Equal suffrage, for example, was achieved quite suddenly during World War I.)

In all these respects and others not mentioned it appears that a modern war offers an opening for the rise of group tensions. It also happens that during such a war the instrumentalities of government are converged upon the conduct of the war and consequently are diverted from the ordinary tasks of reconciling domestic interests. Certain elements of democracy, in other words, are suspended in wartime and to the extent that this occurs one should expect an increase in group friction and conflict. It has been the tendency of modern wars to carry an increment of revolutionary content. The chief difficulty involved in all of this derives from the fact that it is a modern manifestation and is not characteristic of past history. Thus it happens that we have been "caught" by surprise. We expected national unity and encountered national disunity. Once we have accustomed ourselves to this new element of modern wars, we should be able to make proper allowances and seek appropriate adjustments.

4. Finally, social tensions increase when a society is confronted with the necessity of adapting itself to new ideas and movements. A social movement may be described for our purposes as (a) an idea struggling for expression and demonstration, (b) a human need for which the new idea stands as symbol, (c) a body of proponents, (d) the emergence of new types of leadership, and (e) the rise of an opposition. Each of these components of a social movement precip-

itates a special tension and the combination of these lesser tensions emerges ultimately as conflict on a national scale.

A social movement may be said to represent an adaptive compulsion. We know that we must somehow come to grips with the new idea, that is, make an adaptation to its claims. At the same time, the very demands inherent in the new movement generate in us apprehensions and fears. Those who seem to require a high degree of certainty will instinctively reject the new idea and seek solace in an imagined security of the past. Those who shrink from all forms of conflict will postpone their personal adaptations. Until the new idea has broken through the crust of habit and has opened the way for calm experimentation there will be tension. One way of preparing one's self for meeting tensions of this variety is, obviously, that of understanding the nature of the imminent ideas and movements. With this notion in mind I am now suggesting a series of new social movements which seem to me to be causing uneasiness and tension among American citizens.

Social security represents a new idea and a new claim. It has now become so persistent that it seems to me fair to assume that all modern societies, especially those already industrialized, will henceforth be compelled to guarantee a basic social security to their citizens as the price of stability and peace. In this country the idea of mutualized security runs counter to our historic individualism. Consequently, we are bound to experience considerable stress and strain as we move in the direction of this goal. A bill expanding our present social security law will soon be debated in Congress and I anticipate a bitter struggle both within the halls of Congress and in the forum of public debate.

Racial equality is not a new claim but until recently there has been no world-wide coalescence of this demand. We now know that we cannot postpone this problem. We now know that the yellow and brown and black peoples of the earth do not trust us, and we also know that we, the so-called white race, are the minority group, that in fact the colored races outnumber us almost three to one. A compulsive adaptation to the needs of the colored peoples of this world is now upon us. We Americans will, no doubt, experience great difficulty in connection with this problem and primarily because we have a guilty conscience. It is because of our deep-seated feeling of guilt that we resort so easily to violence when racial tensions become acute.

Economic and social planning is a phrase which denotes one of the most important, if not the most important, movement of our time. It not only runs counter to older conceptions of free enterprise and self-reliance but also to our traditional notion of democracy itself. The illustrations we have thus far seen of planning have been conducted under the aegis of political dictatorships. It is not unusual, therefore, to discover that, whenever this idea obtrudes, there is an immediate sense of tension. The chief difficulty, as I view the matter, derives from a fundamental misunderstanding. Opponents of planning regard the idea and its claims as being ideological in origin. But this is not true. The chief compulsion leading to planning is a derivative of science and technology. Each application of technology to the physical environment tends to weaken and finally to destroy automatic or natural controls. Consequently, each extension of science and technology calls for an extension of conscious control. The question is no longer one of planning *versus* non-planning but rather whether we can have planning and democracy too. It is my firm conviction that there is no essential incompatibility between planning and democracy. It is rather an accident of history that such planning as we have thus far witnessed has been a function of dictatorships.

If, however, we are to make successful accommodations to the requirements of planning, we shall be obliged to sharpen our democratic tools and perhaps invent some new ones. The key to democratic procedures is participation. If we are to operate a democracy that is an instrument for attaining the highest use of our resources and at the same time is a protector of freedom, we shall all need to live in a more intimate relationship with government. If we are not to drift toward planning "from the top down," we must see that the "bottom" is both active and intelligent. In the meantime, as we continue to debate this issue there will be numerous and perplexing tensions to confront.

World collaboration versus isolationism is, perhaps, the most fateful of all the issues which the American people will be called upon to decide in this generation. We stand at the moment wholly unprepared for this great decision both in mind and in spirit. At the close of this war we shall probably be the strongest military power in the world, if not in all history. We will be especially strong in those respects which distinguish modern from traditional warfare; namely, in technical equipment. We must assume also that nationalism will be a powerful sentiment, particularly in the victorious nations. If the alliances created for prosecuting the war continue throughout the period of transition and well into the period of the peace, there may be a good prospect for the organization of the world in such manner as to preclude future aggressions. If these alliances weaken or are allowed to be broken, the United States will, it seems to me, move toward isolation. The new isolationism is militant, prepared and in possession of many important channels of communication. Its program is designed to meet the expected demands of the returning soldiers; namely, their deep need for peace. The isolationists will offer them peace in the form of American isolation plus the maintenance of the strongest military equipment in the world. They will insist that this program will protect us from future involvement in war. The fallacy of this argument is patent; if we become and try to remain the strongest military power in the world, what will other nations do? Obviously, if we are the object to be feared, they will form combinations against us.

Anyone who senses the present mood and temper of the American people (December, 1943) will be aware of the fact that the coming struggle regarding our future role in world affairs is likely to become one of the epic conflicts of our history. To confront a typical forum audience these days is to become acutely aware of the divergent streams of thought and feeling with respect to this issue. The tensions are evident but are at this moment held in check. As the war moves toward a conclusion we shall witness the unfolding of a divergence which will, so I believe, place upon the nation one of the severest strains of its career.

It must be clear to the reader that each of the issues discussed above involves moral considerations. These are not merely questions of expediency; on the contrary, these are questions which will compel us to choose between right and wrong, good and evil. The democratic idea imposes upon its adherents a peculiar type of morality. If, for example, our decisions carry us away from privilege and toward an enlarging equity, we will then have the assurance that we are moving in the direction of democratic morality. We ought now to be examining all of our existing commitments to the world from this ethical viewpoint, inclusive of the Atlantic Charter, the United Nations Declaration, the Moscow, Cairo, and Teheran agreements, as well as our Food Conference and United Nations Relief and Rehabilitation contracts. If we can find it in our hearts and minds to take a high position in which our national interests are equated with firm moral convictions, we may demonstrate both to ourselves and to the world that these present tensions constitute the test of our will and courage.

IV

GROUP DISCRIMINATION AND CULTURE CLASH

BY

JOSEPH S. ROUCEK, PH.D.

Chairman, Department of Political Science and Sociology, Hofstra College

In the spring of 1943 we saw Americans fighting one another in the shipyards of Mobile and in the streets of Newark and Los Angeles; Americans striking in Detroit and Brooklyn because they resented the presence of other Americans working beside them; Americans protesting that Americans in concentration camps were being "coddled"; Americans insulting other Americans before the House Immigration Committee; and Americans carrying on a civil war, known as the "zoot-suit" war, against Americans in Los Angeles. In each instance the question of racial and cultural discrimination was involved—the Americans under verbal or physical attack being also Negroes, Mexicans, Japanese, and Chinese—and every skirmish was an Axis victory, militarily and ideologically.

We have embattled minorities within the United States which are minorities because their skins are not white—the "non-vanishing" Indians, the Chinese, the Mexicans—within our borders; our Japanese hostages, the amazing Hawaiian melting pot, our unhappy Puerto Rican wards, our Filipinos, together with the all-pervasive Negro problem. Their problems are not pretty pictures simply because we have refused to face them and declined to treat them in a statesmanlike way and have preferred to ignore them whenever we can. Many people are irritated that one of the many unexpected impacts of this war has been to put these problem citizens of ours straight to the front.

The Goebbels propaganda has not been wholly unskillful in pointing out this unhappy side of our national life. The difficulty, of course, is that we are pretending in this war to save democracy, when we have not given democracy to all these millions within our borders. Our sins are catching up with us in the most surprising way, and most of us do not like it and think discussions of it should be postponed until we have smashed Hitler, Italy, and the Japanese, and occupied their capitals. There is, however, another school which thinks that we cannot hope to win in this war unless we live up to our pretensions and put our house in order.

The writer, for one, belongs to the latter school.

For the group discrimination problem is, in fact, in the background of the present war. We can ask ourselves: "Are we fighting the war as a people?" In a concrete and limited sense, the answer seems to be: "No, we are not!" Indeed, the newspapers are filled daily with evidence that we are not. There is the Negro question and the canker of anti-Semitism. These are founded upon "racial" prejudice. There are other divisions—labor and capital, agriculture and labor, big business and small business. We are not concerned with them here. We are interested only in the divisions promoting group discrimination, based on cultural differences. In this respect, it seems that the answer is definitely: "No, we are not fighting this war as a people."

That is the great weakness of our home front, a weakness which is serious in a strong people seeking victory. China, Russia, know very definitely what they are fighting for as a people. We, too, once knew. We celebrated (in 1943) the liberty we won 160 years ago. Then we fought as a people and knew what we were fighting for. We, in our present crisis, know as a nation what we are fighting *against*. But, as a people, we are not at all certain what we are fighting *for*. Certainly, we have done more fighting on behalf of group discrimination than for group tolerance and understanding. The events of 1943 certified to this assumption.

INTERNATIONAL IMPLICATIONS OF OUR HOME DISCRIMINATION

The social discrimination practices against America's minorities have their own international implications. Can Brazilians ever be wholly *simpatico* with us so long as we suppress a large Negro minority in the United States? American Negroes are quite aware of the sharp difference in treatment afforded members of their race in the Western Hemisphere outside the United States. Let us not forget that the overwhelming majority of our anti-Axis allies belongs to the colored races. While there are 12,000,000 Negroes in the United States, there are 37,000,000 persons of African origin in the Western Hemisphere (including those of the United States), with large concentrations in the West Indies, Brazil, and other areas. While there are 390,000 Indians in the United States and Alaska there are 30,000,000 Indians in Central and South America.[1]

In fact, "the growing identification of the American Negro with nonwhite people all over the world," writes Horace R. Cayton, "is no figment of Nazi propaganda."[2] Throughout the colored world there are undercurrents watching the changing status of colored as well as nonwhite people. There are many evidences of a growing sense of solidarity between American Negroes and the peoples of India.[3]

The Nazi and the Japanese propagandists have made quite a serious effort to make capital out of the racial problems the world over. Tokyo radio programs daily send their broadcasts over Asia in their campaign to drive out the white man, and Germany has been helping Japan to stir up race hatred in Malaya, India, and the Philippines. The Nazi concern over the status of the American Indian would appear to be utterly fantastic—except that the Nazi broadcasts, timed to counteract Good Neighbor Programs from the United States, harp upon the treatment accorded the Indian in the United States, and are aimed at the Indian element of the republics of Central and South America.

In 1943, by radio, in leaflets and posters, Japanese propagandists were hammering at Chinese morale by pointing out:[4]

[1] Carey McWilliams, *Brothers under the Skin* (Boston: Little, Brown, 1943), p. 14; the "Introduction," pp. 3–49, is an excellent survey of the international implications of our racial problem.

[2] *Ibid.*, p. 19.

[3] *Ibid.*, p. 20.

[4] *Time*, XLI, 24 (June 4, 1943), p. 19; see: Saul K. Padover, "Japanese Race Propaganda," *Public Opinion Quarterly*, VII, 2 (Summer, 1943), pp. 191–210.

America is China's ally. Americans say they love and admire the Chinese. But can you go to America, can you become citizens? No. Americans don't want you. They just want you to do their fighting. Their Exclusion Act names you and says you are unfit for American citizenship. If Generalissimo Chiang really has influence in America, why has he not had this stigma erased from American law? There will be no such discrimination against you in the Greater East Asia Co-Prosperity Sphere.

The Immigration Act of 1924 banned all Oriental immigration. What particularly humiliates the Chinese is that, among all Orientals, including Japanese, they alone are specifically singled out by name in United States law as undesirable citizens. The Chinese Exclusion Act of 1882 was the result of a California labor surplus (thousands of coolies helped build the United States railroads). But the Act, long obsolete, is still on the books.

These facts had the United States Congress on a tough spot. Before the House Immigration Committee were, in 1943, three bills to modify or repeal Chinese exclusion. If the Committee failed to vote out one of the bills, Chinese feelings would be deeply hurt. If the bills were reported and passed, the A. F. of L., American Legion, and Veterans of Foreign Wars would be very angry with Congress. And if the Bills were reported out and rejected, matters would be still worse: it would be a slap in the face of China, whose morale was already suffering from six years of war. A famed Catholic prelate, Bishop Paul Yu-pin, told the Committee:

Should thousands of tanks and airplanes from America to China not be forthcoming immediately, the Chinese people and soldiers perhaps will understand that Allied strategy of global warfare dictates otherwise for the time. But should your honorable committee look unfavorably upon these bills before you today, then I assure you that my country and my people will not be able to understand. It will be a great blow to our morale in China and do irreparable harm to the Allied cause.[5]

The discriminatory aspects of our minorities problem is not only an international problem *par excellence;* it is also a problem which includes a much larger number of minorities than we are usually aware of.

[5] *Ibid.*, p. 20.

THE "FORGOTTEN" MINORITIES OF OUR TERRITORIES

To most Americans the outlying territories and possessions of this country have never seemed an integral part of the nation; much less have the peoples of these territories been thought of as fellow citizens. Only World War II has brought these possessions directly within the orbit of our day-to-day thinking.

In addition to Hawaii and Puerto Rico, we have Alaska (made up of Eskimos and Indians), the Virgin Islands (most of whose inhabitants are colored), the Panama Canal Zone (with a large number of "mixed" and "colored" persons), Guam (21,000 out of 22,000 residents belonging to the native Indonesian stock, known as *Chamorros*), and American Samoa (most of whose population are native Polynesians). These groups may be small numerically contrasted to the totals of the population of the United States, but their existence seriously complicates the larger minority problem in America. We have no adopted general policy for the treatment of these minorities, no adequate administrative apparatus to cope with the problem; we have not related these people in our thinking, much less in our policy, to the colored minorities resident on the mainland. We are hardly even aware, for instance, that the United States gave unrestricted access, by right of citizenship, to our fellow citizens of Puerto Rico, but that these 100,000 Puerto Ricans are social outcasts in New York's Harlem, and that the dissatisfaction of the Harlem Puerto Ricans finds an echo in the island and among the large Negro population throughout the West Indies, the Caribbean, and Central and South America.

GROUP DISCRIMINATION DEFINED

Group, that is, social discrimination is "the unequal treatment of equals, either by bestowal of favors or the imposition of burdens." [6] Says Johnson: "It carries with it the idea of arbitrariness, of unfairness, and of injustice. It involves the inclusion or exclusion of groups or individuals by an infinite number of arbitrary lines of demarcation

[6] Charles S. Johnson, *Patterns of Negro Segregation* (New York: Harper, 1943), pp. xvii–xviii.

drawn on the basis of the most varied marks of similarity or dissimilarity. Differential treatment of individuals based upon accepted differences in rank or status is the result of a similar process."

This definition is important for our discussion because of the conflict between the theory of democratic institutions, which grants equality to all, and the sanctions in the mores supporting and justifying unequal treatment of theoretical equals, with the resulting cultural conflicts leading to social and economic discrimination and disadvantage for the minority or less dominant group, and generally to a lack of teamwork in various relations. By cultural differences we mean here differences in religious outlook, in mores, manners, and culture patterns in general.

It is important to keep in mind that America's population is by no means a homogeneous group, and hence we are confronted by an excessive number of discriminatory practices. Social and cultural distinctions of a significant character stratify our population, and the divisions suggest the differential values of these groups as culture bearers. Hence the patterns of social discrimination appear also to vary according to the social and economic factors dominant in various regions. There are great variations in the customary social discriminatory practices from one locality to another. In our case, we are not interested in the endless variety of social and economic distinctions, but only in those affecting the majority-minority relationships in the United States. When minority peoples identify their status and destiny with the conditions of their race or minority characteristics, they become minority or race conscious and take on the characteristics of a minority group.

DEGREES OF SOCIAL DISCRIMINATION

In one way or another, America's minorities are excluded from full participation in the life of community and the conduct of the state. This immediately raises the problem of the relation of this circumstance to the democratic theory of the state, which assumes complete participation of all who are capable of functioning economically and socially as members of society. The fact remains that the actual practices of the dominant majority are, for whatever reason, in direct conflict with the ideals and professed objectives of the ideology underlying the concept of the *United* States. The theory of the democratic state assumes, in regard to America's minorities, a degree of cultural assimilation corresponding to their equal status in citizenship. In actual practice, however, the democratic theory is frankly qualified by the dominant group's value judgment of assimilability. Minority groups that are physically and culturally similar to the dominant pattern or ideal are acceptable; other groups, which differ markedly from the norm are less acceptable. In their case adjustment or accommodation within the framework of the democratic society is demanded rather than assimilation or just the legal status of citizenship.

The extreme case of social discrimination is the situation of the American Indian, who is segregated, thus being put totally outside the cultural framework of American society. The Negro provides the most distinct and clearly defined racial segregation in the South, while elsewhere there is little professed segregation but a subtle and persistent discrimination in practically all areas of life, particularly in the economic sphere. The Mexicans present a mixed pattern, depending upon the social judgment of several sections of America with respect to assimilability. For instance, in California the Mexican laborer is classed racially as nonwhite and, thus, automatically segregated, a situation caused by aversion to color, social pressure against intermixture with an "inferior" race, disdain of the conqueror for the conquered, hatred of frontiersmen for those who are or who have been at some time in their way, the revulsion of the Protestant and Puritanical Yankee against Roman Catholicism and Latin folkways, and contempt of the higher economic class for the lower.[7] In New Mexico, on the other hand, the Spanish-speaking minority is not socially segregated and ostracized; there these people are regarded as white (by census definition at least), and particularly in recent years because their good will is now essential to hemispherical solidarity.

The Orientals are singularly segregated, although the situation in regard to the Chinese is changing because of the war fortunes, as we shall see later. But, on the whole, the social segregation in regard to the Orientals applies most commonly to residential areas, schools,

[7] B. Shrieke, *Alien Americans* (New York: Viking Press, 1936), p. 54.

churches, and various semipublic and public institutions and services. In their case, social unassimilability is associated with political unacceptability for citizenship.

Then there are three groups which are acceptable for citizenship, but upon whom the shadow of segregation falls sometimes and social discrimination nearly all the time: the foreign-born and their American-born children, the Jews, and the Negroes.[8]

NEGRO RESENTMENT AGAINST DISCRIMINATION

In the field of group discrimination, the Negro problem is one of the most serious and important aspects of our national situation. Never was there a more complicated problem, never one whose roots go so deeply into the past and into actual social and economic conditions of today.

Since Pearl Harbor, national friction over the status of the Negro population has been on the increase. Many Negroes have been angry at the discrimination against them in the Army and Navy, and above all in the war industries; to them their position as steerage passengers on a ship of state headed for democracy for all people seems cruelly ironical. Feeling among them seethed, died down, and since 1943 has seethed again. Their attitude galls and scars many Southern whites; and there have been times when wild rumors of Negro uprisings swept through Southern towns—rumors some of which must have been deliberately invented—and threatened to explode in open race warfare.

THE SHAME OF DETROIT'S RIOTS

In the summer of 1943, Detroit had the bloodiest race riots the country has had since 1919. White and black Detroiters slugged, clubbed, gouged, stoned, kicked, stabbed, and shot each other until 31 were dead, more than 600 injured, and 1,800 arrested. After several thousand soldiers in full battle dress put down the riots, a fact-finding

[8] Within this general framework of social discrimination there are, in turn, numerous variations; see: E. S. Bogardus, *Immigration and Race Attitudes* (Boston: D. C. Heath, 1928), p. 26, and Maurice H. Krout, "Periodic Change in Social Distance," *Sociology and Social Research,* XXVII, 5 (May–June, 1943), pp. 339–351; Joseph S. Roucek, "Social Attitudes of Native-Born Children of Foreign-Born Parents," *Sociology and Social Research,* XXII, 2 (November–December, 1937), pp. 139–150.

committee appointed by Governor Kelly of Michigan went to work to determine its causes.[9] Group discrimination looms large among the causes: (1) Detroit's abominable housing situation which condemns thousands of white and Negro war workers to living in slums, tents, and trailers; (2) the tremendous migration of white and Negro war workers from the south since 1940; (3) "race" strikes and friction in war plants (in June, 1943, 20,000 Packard workers walked out because three Negro workers were upgraded to the assembly line); and (4) juvenile rowdyism, which had increased during the war. (In June, 1943, 100 white and Negro youths fought a pitched battle in a Detroit playground.) "Although the riot was definitely a victory for Adolf Hitler and other enemies of the United States, there was no evidence that it had been planned by foreign agents, local Fascists, or anyone else. It broke out suddenly on a hot Sunday night, and its basic cause was an old, ugly fact in United States life; prejudice and misunderstanding between the white and black races.[10]

The efforts to pin the responsibility upon the Nazi agents, upon the Ku-Klux-Klan, and similar organizations showed the usual tendency to adopt a superficial procedure and to deal with effects, not causes. The real cause lies much deeper: in the ignorance, economic and even dietary backgrounds of both the Negroes and the whites from the South who were primarily responsible for the disorders. Suddenly into Detroit, for industrial and economic reasons, thousands of workers were imported from the Deep South. In the case of the Negroes, most of them had lived all their lives upon starvation wages, with rarely more than a quarter at a time in their pockets. Many of them were illiterate. All of them were accustomed to Jim Crow laws and severe racial discrimination and restrictions. Suddenly they were "freed." They had money. There were no Jim Crow laws. In a new and different world they were rich beyond anything they had ever dreamed of. The change was too great, the necessity for adjustment too violent.

[9] For the photographic evidence of the riots, see: *Life*, XV, 1 (July 5, 1943), pp. 93–100. A. M. Lee and N. D. Humphrey, *Race Riot* (New York: Dryden Press, 1943), is a valuable report on the Detroit riots.

[10] Life, *op. cit.*, p. 93.

But beside them were brought from the South thousands of indigent and very often ignorant white workers, most of them accustomed to earnings and standards of living little, if at all, better than those of the Negroes. These were men who for generations had known insufficient food and little or no education. Their only claim to superiority or in some cases even to human dignity was on the basis of color, of different race, on the basis of group discrimination. It is too often overlooked in dealing with the Negro problem that the bitterest prejudices exist among the whites of low economic positions and standards of living. All too often it serves as a salve to their own sense of bewilderment, resentment, and inferiority. Placing these two racial elements, both suddenly prosperous, side by side in the strange unnatural environment of an overcrowded industrial town could produce only an explosion. It is probably not the last explosion we shall see. Certainly it was evil but realistic evidence that we are not fighting the war as a people. The solution of our Negro problem with all its complications can be reached only slowly, gradually, by evolution. It is, sadly enough, a slow process.

SOCIAL DISCRIMINATION EVIDENCED IN HARLEM RIOT

The riot in Harlem in August, 1943, was a social explosion in a powder keg that has been years in the filling. It was rooted in the Negro's dissatisfaction with his racial status, not only in Harlem but all over the country, and exhibited in his efforts, sometimes intelligent and extreme, to break down the economic and social discrimination, barriers and frustrations which at times seem unbearable. It was not a race riot: at no time was there fighting between Negro and white groups as there was in Los Angeles and Detroit. On that point there was almost universal agreement among Negroes and whites. But to dismiss the affair as merely an example of hooliganism and vandalism would completely dodge the issue. There is no question that rioters, hoodlums though they may have been, were protesting in their own way against the many discriminations which Negroes suffer, even in New York. "The war has awakened a new sense of racial consciousness among Negroes all over the country, but in no place has it struck so deeply as in Harlem," commented *The Nation*.[11]

"The men who have been drafted from Harlem have been particularly outraged by the segregation and discrimination practiced in the Army and Navy, and their protests have fanned the already existing fires of discontent caused by job discrimination, bad housing, high rents, high prices, insufficient recreational and educational opportunities, and occasional police brutality. . . . The long-range task of giving Harlem a fair share in the employment, education, health, and recreation facilities of the nation has not been met by city, state, or federal government." [12]

OTHER NATIONAL RESULTS OF DISCRIMINATION

But the shame was not Detroit's and Harlem's alone in 1943. Their outbreaks were a symptom of a racial tension festering all over the country. There were also serious outbreaks in Mobile (Alabama) and Beaumont (Texas). There were minor clashes in El Paso and Port Arthur (Texas), Springfield (Massachusetts), Hubbard (Ohio), and even in Britain, where the American Negro soldiers and military police battled in the streets of a northwestern town. And the Axis propagandists made the most of this grist for their ceaseless mill: "It is a singular fact," said a Japanese broadcast, "that supposedly civilized Americans in these times deny the Negroes the opportunity to engage in respectable jobs, the right of access to the restaurants, theaters, or the same train connections as themselves and periodically will run amuck to lynch Negroes individually or to slaughter them wholesale—old men, women, and children alike in race wars like the present one." [13]

[11] Editorial, *The Nation,* CLVII, 7 (August 14, 1943), p. 170.

[12] Russell J. Porter, "Harlem Unrest Traced to Long-Standing Ills," *The New York Times,* August 8, 1943, quoted Lester B. Granger, executive secretary of the National Urban League, who was convinced that much could be done if there were better leadership among both the whites and Negroes who are actively interested in the problem, that the Negro leadership should return to the more moderate hands in which it was held before 1934 and 1935, when Communists and other extremist advocates of "mass pressure" took over, and that the white leadership should include more practical businessmen and labor leaders and fewer sentimentalists, professional liberals, and the like.

[13] "Festering Tension," *Newsweek,* XXII, 1 (July 5, 1943), pp. 35–36.

At the root of it all lay the vast sociological complex that makes for bigotry and social discrimination on both sides. Some of them we have already noted. But let us also note that some of the Negroes, too, turned arrogant. They not only had more money and freedom than they had ever enjoyed at home in the South, but others grew desperate and despairing as they saw their sons and brothers enter the fighting forces, while discrimination against them mounted at home. Negroes felt that the Administration, while vaunting its Four Freedoms before the world, did little for their race at home.

Behind all the trouble, so far as the threat of overt action was concerned, has been an impatient, irresistible drive of the Negroes, on the one hand, for a fuller realization of the equality which has long been promised to them, but just as long denied; and, on the other hand, a stubborn, deepening, and in some places broadening, resistance of the whites to that very aim. The Negro is taking this occasion to make a determined drive, come what may, for his "rights." One faction of the Negro leaders is insisting not merely on rights comparable or even equal to the whites; they want the "same" rights, which they translate to mean the privilege to use the same facilities as the whites —the same hotels, theatres, night clubs, etc. Segregation, the word and all it stands for, has become anathema to the Negro, so far as he is represented by his more vocal leaders of today.

OUR SPANISH-SPEAKING AND CHINESE MINORITIES

The native-born Mexicans, Chinese, and Japanese of foreign or mixed parentage comprise only a little over two per cent of the second-generation population. But in many ways their problems as members of the second generation are both unique and important; moreover, the fact that they are highly concentrated in certain sections of the country causes them to assume a greater significance within the second-generation population than their absolute numbers would warrant.

THE DISCRIMINATION AGAINST AMERICAN CHINESE

The Chinese question has lost its economic significance, and tolerant indifference to the Chinese has taken the place of hatred on the part of the Americans. But, so far as the American-Chinese are concerned, the problem has grown steadily worse, for tolerance is not acceptance, and indifference is not assimilation. Thus the relations of the Americans and the Chinese have become symbiotic rather than social. They live side by side, but in two entirely different worlds; their relations are "cold, formal, and commercial." [14]

These unsatisfactory social relations result in deplorable conditions in the various Chinatowns. Because of the enforced segregation San Francisco's Chinatown, although a picturesque place to visit, is cursed with the problem of overcrowding, congestion, and is "San Francisco's main slum area," in the words of the San Francisco Housing Authority.[15]

The situation of the American Chinese is truly paradoxical. In California, for instance, the Chinese are perhaps the oldest immigrants in the state, most of them belonging to the second, third, and fourth generation. They had lived there much longer, for example, than the Armenians and the Portuguese. Yet they had failed to win for themselves a comparable place in the social, economic, and political life of the state, simply because they have been the victims of a caste system similar to that which prevails in the Deep South. "It has been this caste system, rather than any inherent biological factor, that has prevented full assimilation. As a matter of fact, the Chinese have actually changed biologically; it has been their social position which has remained static." [16] They cannot marry outside their own group; they can attend American schools and higher institutions of learning but after graduation can specialize only in washing dishes. Up to the end of 1938, the Oriental Division of the United States Employment Service in San Francisco reported that 90 per cent of its placements of the American-born Chinese were for service workers, chiefly in the culinary trades. As late as June, 1940,

[14] Carey McWilliams, *Brothers under the Skin* (Boston: Little, Brown, 1943), p. 99. See also: Rose Zeligs, "Influencing Children's Attitudes Toward the Chinese," *Sociology and Social Research,* XXVI (November–December, 1941), pp. 126–138; Robert W. O'Brien, "Status of the Chinese in the Mississippi Delta," *Social Forces,* XIX (March 1941), pp. 1–5.

[15] *Ibid.,* p. 101.

[16] *Ibid.,* p. 102.

the service reported that, with few exceptions, most firms discriminated against Chinese in employment, although most of them are well educated and many have received special training.[17]

This situation has produced a chronic crisis of the second, third, and fourth generation. "Actually," wrote White in 1941, "only the face of Chinatown is bright. The heart of Chinatown is frustrated, perplexed, discontented, restless. It represents a 'melting pot' which has 'let the people down.'"[18] Although numerous sociologists have always noted that the Chinese had been able to boast of one of the lowest crime rates of any immigrant groups in America, by 1940 observers began to note the appearance of factors making for a sharp increase in juvenile delinquency, related intimately to a growing sense of frustration, most noticeable prior to Pearl Harbor.[19]

THE STRANGE CASE OF OUR SPANISH-SPEAKING MINORITY

Of the Mexican immigrants, most of whom are migratory workers, much has been written.[20] One of the most important facts is that they are socially ostracized and sharply set apart from the resident white communities. Thus the Mexican immigrant continues to speak Spanish, to live among his own group, and to follow his own mode of living. "Not even in the most superficial sense does he have an opportunity to become acculturated."[21]

The situation is bad in regard to the Mexican migratory workers, but is definitely worse when we view the conditions faced by the

[17] A few of these had, however, made themselves known; Dr. Chien-Shiung Wo is recognized as one of the most brilliant young physicians in America.

[18] "Crisis in Chinatown," by Nate R. White, *Christian Science Monitor,* February 1, 1941.

[19] Fortunately, since Pearl Harbor, Chinese began to be placed in positions as stenographers, timekeepers, welders, carpenters, shipyard workers, and aircraft workers. As the younger Chinese moved into the American community, "antique shops and chop-suey restaurants and hand laundries began to close their doors," reports McWilliams (*op. cit.,* p. 106).

[20] Cf.: Carey McWilliams, *op. cit.,* chapter III, "The Forgotten Mexican," pp. 114–146; E. S. Bogardus, *The Mexican in the United States* (Los Angeles: University of Southern California Press, 1934); Jovita Gonzales de Mireles, "Latin Americans," pp. 497–509, in Francis J. Brown & Joseph S. Roucek, *Our Racial and National Minorities* (New York: Prentice-Hall, 1937), and bibliography, pp. 832–833.

[21] C. McWilliams, *op. cit.,* p. 119.

American-born Spanish-speaking minority in New Mexico, and the sizable Mexican colonies in such communities as Chicago, Detroit, Flint, Gary, and Bethlehem. These minority settlements are segregated from the rest of the community almost as effectively as the Negro. Although the members are not kept apart from the Anglo-Americans in lavatories, waiting rooms, and public vehicles, as is the Negro, their poverty and low wages separate them in the poorest sections of the city and New Mexico.

It is a strange situation particularly in regard to the Hispanos of New Mexico where in 1940 some 221,740 New Mexicans listed Spanish as their monther tongue out of the total population of 531,818. Descendants from the colonies established there in the Rio Grande Valley since 1540 became the citizens of the United States following the war of 1846; their culture pattern is based on a primitive agricultural economy, language, customs, and technology which even up to date is really that of sixteenth-century Spain.[22] Although these Hispanos are all citizens and constitute a numerical majority in New Mexico, nevertheless, the great mass of them remain a severely handicapped social and economic group. "While due recognition must be given to the successful manner in which some members of the group have adapted themselves to the new environment, it is to be observed that the great masses of the people constitute a severely handicapped social and economic minority. Generally speaking, their status is one of privation and want, of cultural inadequacy, and of bewilderment. Neglected for more than two hundred years as Spanish colonials and Mexicans, their cultural situation was not greatly improved by the territorial regime. In fact, the little improvement that took place through the limited educational efforts that were made in their behalf was more than offset by the social and economic decline that resulted from the influx of new peoples and of a new economic order." [23] Without assigning their highest illiteracy rates, the worst public-health conditions, the worst housing, the lowest in-

[22] Glen Leonard and G. P. Loomis, *Culture of a Contemporary Rural Community, El Cerrito, New Mexico* (Washington, D.C.: U.S. Department of Agriculture, Rural Life Studies: 1), is a revealing study of this situation.

[23] George I. Sanchez, *Forgotten People, A Study of New Mexicans* (Albuquerque, N.M.: The University of New Mexico Press, 1940), p. 27.

come levels, and the most poverty to social discrimination, we may safely assume, on the basis of the available studies,[24] that their low social status is one of the basic causes of their inferior social practices and beliefs which have forced them to live in a traditional way of life that is below current standards. Thus their social status reflects their economic insufficiency, related, in turn, to little chance to learn to use English effectively, the lack of education handicapping them to exercise their political power, and the whole wreckage of their economic life and culture forcing them by their pathetic helplessness to be unprepared for the new order of affairs.[25]

SOCIAL DISCRIMINATION AND "ZOOT-SUIT RIOTS"

Next to the Detroit riots, the "Zoot-Suit Riots" attracted America's attention in 1943. Similar factors as in the Detroit trouble appeared as the factors in Los Angeles. Racial restrictions against housing have crowded a large influx of Mexicans from the South, brought to Los Angeles to work in war plants, into the downtown district known as "Little Tokyo" (occupied formerly by the evacuated Japanese). Many of the Mexican population of almost a quarter of a million (probably one fourth Mexican nationals, three fourths United States citizens) are forced to live in slum conditions. These factors, with some racial discrimination in schools, restaurants, theatres, and the like, are blamed as contributory to a state of mind lending itself readily to crime. Several interesting aspects of social discrimination crop up here. For instance, although some of the youths involved in the riots wore no zoot suits, virtually all were of Mexican descent. The Los Angeles' Chief of Police blamed the press for publicizing zoot-

[24] Sanchez, *op. cit.;* L. S. Tireman, *La Comunidad, Report of the Naube Community School 1937–1942;* Allan G. Harper, Andrew R. Cordova, and Kalervo Oberg, *Man and Resources in the Middle Rio Grande Valley* (both, Albuquerque, N.M.: The University of New Mexico Press, 1943).

[25] We must note here the interest displayed in this minority by the Office of the Coordinator of Inter-American Affairs and the Inter-American Workshop, sponsored by this Office at the New Mexico Highlands University, Las Vegas, and directed by Professor Quincy Guy Burris, on the theory that the elevation of the standards of the New Mexico Spanish-speaking minority could be utilized for the promotion of Inter-American understanding. See: Quincy Guy Burris, "Radio Takes to the Hills," *American Unity,* II (November, 1943), pp. 6–9.

suit gangs and contended that many of the rioters sought principally to get their pictures in the papers. Other observers recognized race prejudice as a factor which led servicemen to beset swarthy civilian youths wherever they saw them. According to Eduardo Quevedo, President of the Coordinating Council for Latin Americans, member of the Citizens' Committee on Latin American Youth, the zoot-suiters represented a basic American problem: the second generation. Their fathers and mothers are still Mexicans at heart.[26] They themselves are Americans—resented and looked down on by other Americans. Jobless, misunderstood in their own homes and unwelcome outside them, they have fallen into the companionship of misery. They dress alike, in the most exaggerated and outlandish costume they can afford: knee-length coats, peg-top trousers, yard-long watch chains, "ducktail" haircuts. But these "pachucos," these "zoot-suit gangs" were only the equivalent of boys' gangs almost anywhere —and particularly of the gangs which are the outgrowth of the "second-generation" problems.

THE BURNING PROBLEM OF THE SECOND GENERATION

The second generation of immigrants, who constitute a population of over 26 million, occupy a unique cultural position in America on account of group discrimination. Usually forced to adjust to two or more different social and cultural worlds, that of their parents, on the one hand, and that of American society on the other, they encounter numerous problems of cultural conflicts and group prejudices. These problems are especially in evidence in the family situations and lie at the root of delinquency and personality maladjustments. Contributory to second-generation problems are the special handicaps inherent in the low socioeconomic status of their parents, the circumscribed character of the immigrant community in which many of them live, and the prejudicial attitude of American society toward minority groups.

We recognize, of course, that many second-generation individuals

[26] "Zoot-Suit War," *Time,* XLI, 25 (June 21, 1943), pp. 18–19. Cf. also: E. S. Bogardus, "Gangs of Mexican-American Youth," *Sociology and Social Research,* XXVIII (September–October, 1943), pp. 55–66.

are well adjusted and have never experienced problems which made them cognizant of their difference from native Americans, or have solved them adequately and successfully. In the study of the adjustment of any group to a social and cultural milieu, a number of positive as well as negative aspects of the situation are important to understand—such as the degree of total adjustment that has been effected by the group, the speed of adjustment with reference to certain elements—*e.g.*, language, family mores, courtship customs, etc., and the ways by which adjustment is achieved.

But the fact remains that the initiation of the second-generation Americans into our democratic life remains one of the acute, although neglected, problems. It has cost us much in maladjustment, in crime, in poverty, and in family disorganization to arrive at the conclusion that this problem should be faced squarely by adequate social policy which would comprehend the needs and aspirations of our social and national minorities.

The second-generation immigrant (or native-born American) enters upon the American scene already burdened with a number of serious handicaps, which are at the root of his problems, the result, in most instances, of foreign background and the attitude of prejudice generally manifested toward the most recent immigrant stock.

Things foreign often lack status in America in many respects, and consequently the children of foreign-born parents often suffer loss of "caste," inner conflict, as well as outward self-consciousness and shame because of their inferior position as members of a foreign group. Indeed, when home and parents are decidedly Old World, the child frequently displays foreign accent or intonation in his English speech, uses foreign idioms and mannerism, lacks graces in "polite" American society. These externals, mere superficial manifestations of cultural background, often persist in the child, especially if he does not have the opportunity of taking part freely in American life outside of the school.

Even in the school, in the numerous instances when the child attends a neighborhood institution, he meets with children of his own or other second-generation groups only, so that his progress is retarded in learning the ways of the larger society. He remains in many conscious ways a product of his environment or at least a recognized member of it. Thus, the more foreign his home, the more difficult it is for him to become assimilated into American life and to feel secure as an accepted member of American society. Since most of our recent immigrants have come from Central-Eastern Europe, we can readily see the implications of the "foreignness" of a large number of our population.

The initial handicap which the second generation must meet because of the foreign birth of their parents appears all the more onerous in view of the fact that those parents find adjustment to American ways an exceedingly slow and difficult process. The overwhelming majority of the foreign-born are never wholly assimilated, and most of them do not at any time achieve more than superficial and partial adjustment, for the familiar culture norms are weighted with the sentiment of loyalty, devotion, justice, and rightness, as well as deeply rooted in the soil of tradition, custom, the inertia. They become so inseparable from the individual's emotional, intellectual, and spiritual nature as often to be considered, contrary to anthropological science, as immutable as racial characteristics.

When these cultural allegiances become interrelated with the political allegiances, such as the tendency of many Italians and Germans to support Mussolini and Hitler, we are confronted with "divided loyalties" that have so long been elements of confusion and danger in American life.[27]

Added to the cultural cleavages between the immigrant's background and American society is his church form and ritual. The immigrant finds it necessary to establish his own church and worship according to his own tradition. When the religion of the immigrant is neither Catholicism nor Protestantism, moreover, his religious position makes it still more difficult for him to assimilate. Many of the Japanese and Chinese, the Jews, and sectarians such as the Molokans are, therefore, in an especially isolated position in American life, comprising, as they do, minority groups within a minority group.

The difficulty which the immigrant faces in adjusting to America

[27] Cf.: Joseph S. Roucek, "Sabotage and America's Minorities," *World Affairs Interpreter*, XIV, 1 (April, 1943), pp. 45–66.

is a function in large part also of his social class and of his standards concerning social status.

Characteristic of a number of immigrant families is that the entire household is solidly organized around the Old World objective, land, to the detriment of the children's status here in America, where standard of living is rated far above the mere possession of real property.

Then comes the struggle which the immigrant experiences with a new language. In numerous instances, he never fully masters English. Related to the handicap of incomplete mastery of English is the immigrant peasant's characteristic lack of education and high illiteracy rate.

All these handicaps reside chiefly in the unbridgeable cultural gulf existing between the background of many of our foreign-born and the American scene. Important to remember for our purpose is that, because of the lack of education, unfamiliarity with American institutions, and the nature of the labor market, many immigrants remain in the cities and find their only employment on the lowest rung of the economic ladder in occupations most subject to the vicissitudes of low wages, irregular employment, and technological displacement. The social significance of this condition is obvious, since in America standard of living is highly important for social status, and unskilled labor is disdained.

The children of these people are seldom able to free themselves entirely from the influence of their parents' foreign origin and from the effects of the inferior social and economic status into which they were born. In addition to the physical effects of the poor home and neighborhood, important are the effects of their dingy homes on the mental outlook. It is difficult to develop home pride under some of the conditions in which these young people must live.

Perhaps the most severe handicap which the second generation faces on first entering upon the American scene is the prejudice of native American society. In America, as we all know, even the most superficial variations from the norm excite scorn and prejudice. In addition, differences in fundamental cultural norms excite more permanent suspicion and hostility, since they create a more significant cleavage and are more tenacious. The Orientals and Mexicans are objects of much more intense bias here than any other people outside of the Negro. With great numerical visibility, prejudice develops.

Without analyzing the complicated factors which promote these prejudices, let us note the elements of group discrimination. Discrimination and intolerance are directed not alone against the alien and foreign-born, but against their children, or, in other words, against those who do not belong by birth to the Protestant, Anglo-Saxon majority. These prejudices often start in the schoolroom. At the age when children brag about their fathers, the elementary-school son of a foreign-born parent learns that his father is a "sheeny," or a "Polock," and thus, an object of scorn or derision. The child of immigrants, like his parents, has to bear the traditional gibes and taunts which children of native Americans have always seemed to learn from the social atmosphere, as it were, and apply to the foreigners and their children. Gibes and jeers lead to blows and severe hazing in many instances. The effect is powerful enough to create very early a division between the second generation and other children, and to mark the sons and daughters of many immigrants with the stigma of inferior status.

To obtain a position within the American business world, the second-generation people often find (prior to our manpower shortage—and even today) that they must, at best, accept blind-alley occupations which offer no opportunity for advancement, or they must do work which white men refuse to do. Those of Jewish parentage find themselves especially handicapped in seeking employment; in keeping with the custom of their people they have in general followed a definite economic tradition, desiring entrance either into small-scale industry and commerce or else the professional and administrative fields. They shun unskilled and even skilled labor, sidetracking to some extent, also, unprofessional wage occupations. In the professions especially, they comprise an overwhelming number of applications in proportion to their population.[28] This particular occupational concentration is the result in large part of the traditional Jewish respect and aspiration for learning. Whereas in Eastern

[28] Irwin Rosen, "The Economic Position of Jewish Youth," *Proceedings* of the National Conference of Jewish Social Welfare, 1936, p. 68.

Europe secular learning was virtually barred to Jews and, instead, religious lore was developed, here in America, with unlimited opportunity for higher education, the Jewish immigrants have far outstripped other ethnic groups and even the native Americans of the same social and economic level, in the number of sons and daughters they send to colleges and professional schools.[29] The results of these economic tendencies have been inevitable. Jewish young people find that competition is severe, since they are too highly concentrated in those vocations and professions which, by virtue of the economic and industrial trends of the day, are undergoing a contraction of opportunity.[30]

Then the serious competition during the recent depression emphasized the always latent force of anti-Semitism, causing even more severe discrimination than usual against Jews in employment. Discrimination is often hidden and is subtly disclosed only to those who must encounter it and in the daily round of looking for a job.[31] Unfortunately, many Jewish young people have developed an almost paranoiac attitude toward the employment situation, and consider every occupational disappointment as an experience in anti-Semitism.[32]

Even when the economic conditions of the second generation have improved, they are still frequently burdened socially because of discrimination. Often they are able to gain social acceptance in the face of prejudice only by means of outstanding individual achievement, ability, or success, and extraordinary charm. The Jew, regardless of his personal and family qualities, is more or less tactfully refused entrance into exclusive social clubs, "first-class" hotels, certain residential districts, and many resorts.[33]

[29] Milton Steinberg, *The Making of the Modern Jew* (1933), pp. 238–240.

[30] Rosen, *op. cit.*, pp. 68–79.

[31] Lewis Browne, *How Odd of God* (1934), pp. 114–115.

[32] Departments of admission in America's higher institutions of learning frequently practice discrimination: Cf.: "Harvard's 'Shifting Committee' on Racial Proportions," *School and Society*, XVI (July 1, 1922), pp. 12–13; Heywood Broun and George Britt, *Christians Only* (1931), pp. 72–124; A. M. Kaplan, "Are Medical Colleges Unfair to Jewish Students," *The Jewish Tribune*, LXXXXVII (August 1, 1930), pp. 3, 13, 14.

[33] Heywood Broun and G. Britt, *Christians Only*, pp. 246–267.

INFERIORITY COMPLEXES OF THE SECOND-GENERATION AMERICANS

Nearly every study concerned with second-generation youth emphasizes that a common personality problem among the children of immigrants is that of a more or less intense feeling of inferiority. Their inferiority feelings are often due, at least in part, to the low status commonly accorded the recent immigrant stock, to the frequent poverty of the home and environment, and to their differences from the general population in a number of conspicuous ways.[34] Not only do they feel inferior in American society because of their foreign background and its attendant handicaps; at the same time, they often possess no compensatory pride in their cultural origin, which frequently eases the burden for their parents. They indulge in compensatory behavior, consciously or subconsciously, to ease their discomfiture. Such behavior frequently takes on the character of aggressiveness and obtrusiveness or of vigorous and insistent assertion of superiority. The "loud" and "tough" young second-generation people, the "noisy painted girls," and "sneering smart alecs" that settlement house directors often encounter are frequently individuals who are merely hiding their sense of inferiority with an air of bravado. As persons of low status, they are "on the defensive." They are often known to make an excessive display of their Americanism in their effort to dissociate themselves from the stigma of their foreign origin; they are anxious and willing to accept the vices and superficialities of American life instead of the fundamental values as their standards of behavior. In their assiduous efforts to become completely Americanized, many second-generation people merely call attention to their "foreignness," for their Americanism is often but a garbled version of the real thing.

[34] Louis Adamic, "Thirty Million New Americans," *Harpers'*, CLXIX (November, 1934), pp. 685–687; Theodore Abel, "Sunderland: A Study of the Changes in the Group Life of Poles in a New England Farming Community," in *Immigrant Farmers and Their Children*, by Edmund de S. Brunner (New York: Doubleday, Doran, 1929), p. 240; Joseph S. Roucek, *Sociological Foundations of Education* (New York: Thomas Y. Crowell, 1942). Dorothy Krall, *The Second Generation Immigrant in America* (doctoral thesis, Yale, 1937) is one of the best surveys of this whole problem.

SOME SOLUTIONS

Speculations on how to solve the second-generation, as well as other aspects of the minority problem, have taken several possible directions. We cannot survey them here; sufficient to state that many of them are romantic and outside the current of world realities.[35] Even Education must not be granted the status of a "cure-for-all." At best, it is a slow and faltering process, subject to all the disadvantages and distortions imposed by a fundamental "will to believe"; namely, the will to believe that the man of a different race or cultural background is a little less human than ourselves. But it is only fair to state that, within its limits, education, if it does not disregard the complexity of causes that underlie our minority problem, can be of considerable help in this respect—although, at the same time, many causes of our plight can be traced to the failure of education.[36]

We must, furthermore, remember that this world cannot be built by sentimentalists, by professional reformers, by soft thinking, and it certainly cannot be rebuilt by those who seek only to return to a prewar world. When changes come for the better they must come from well-organized efforts, promoting primarily ideological convictions that we shall not have a much better world until ignorance and group discrimination are destroyed. There is only one way of destroying them—by reconditioning our ideological reasoning, based on unreasoning prejudices, myths, and fairy tales.

Notes Dr. Johnson: "It is well to observe that traditional racial practices and ideologies which have developed over centuries cannot usually be dissolved within a decade. Since most racial attitudes and all prejudices are nonrational, they are seldom affected by reason or even by humanitarian doctrine. The forces most likely to effect changes in the future are those which gradually have been eroding custom and the idiosyncrasies of the racial etiquette during recent decades." [37]

[35] Some of the solutions are described by Joseph S. Roucek, *op. cit.*, and Dorothy Krall, *op. cit.*

[36] For this sociological aspect of Education as a discipline, see: Joseph S. Roucek, "The Essence of Educational Sociology," pp. 1–25, in *Sociological Foundations of Education.*

[37] Charles S. Johnson, *Patterns of Negro Segregation*, p. 319.

The vital importance of securing equal rights for all men, regardless of their cultural differences or their ancestry, is recognized by all serious thinkers who are giving thought to the survival of this democracy. The problem of harmonizing the living together of persons belonging to different ethnic, linguistic, religious, and cultural groups must be solved if this democracy is to prove that Hitler's racial theories were wicked illusions and false doctrines.

Pearl Buck has told us in ringing accents that the race barriers must be destroyed. Wendell Willkie reports that Stalin told him one of the ends we are fighting for is the end of racial exclusiveness, and Mr. Willkie asks what person in the United Nations can find anything in Stalin's statement to which to object. We are actually told that Japanese resentment at our exclusion laws, smoldering for years, burst into flame at Pearl Harbor, and that if we are sincere in our war aims, we will abrogate our old and well-intrenched policy and remove that bar to yellow and brown immigration. This, then, should be our legal and social policy, designed to eliminate discrimination at home and in international relations.

We have in this country a widespread feeling, if not belief, that we are a definitely superior people and that we are so through a combination of our efforts and genius, our economic good fortune, and because there is something especially fine about the American character. Now, as in any government, especially in a democracy, policy, at least permanent, enduring policy, comes only from the great mass and feeling of the people as a whole, so it is important that as a whole nation we should see ourselves not just in our national self-sufficiency, but in relation to the rest of the world. Our education, both clerical and secular, has too often led us into the vague assumption that history and civilization began with the founding of Christendom, and that the history of the Western World and of the white race is the only history of any importance.

Thus the Chinese are endlessly puzzled by the contrast between the practical good will of the American people who have contributed and still are contributing to them a stream of money, food, and medical supplies, and the fact that at the same time we neglect to send weapons of war which are so desperately needed and delay in nullifying an Exclusion Act which is insulting to them and which in actual practice is no more than a gesture in any case.[38] In this respect, we obviously need quite a lot of straightening of our logical reasoning.

FUTURE STEPS IN CULTURAL PLURALISM

Since culture conflicts are inherent in all forms of social life, cultural integration is beyond the bounds of possibility. In fact, there is no reason to suppose that it would be desirable. But we can do three definite things in order to reduce our group discrimination. First, our culture change does not have to be left to the winds of chance, but can be directed along the lines which appear most desirable at the present time. Second, in order to be able to guide it rationally and intelligently, we must gather as much empiric knowledge on the problem of racial relations as possible. Third, by knowing where we want to go and by having enough scientific information about the most pressing aspects of this problem, we can take steps to reduce these culture conflicts.

Without analyzing all the possibilities involved in our premise, let us propose as the first concrete step the rewriting of our textbooks. Nearly all our American history will have to be rewritten.[39] Most of it has been based on the ideology emphasizing the Anglo-Saxon and Puritanical impress on our civilization. We acknowledge, of course, that America's civilization arose from the thirteen colonies which revolted against England. But these covered only a small portion of the present territory of the country, and included also Dutch and Swedish settlements. Since 1783 the United States has grown mostly by the acquisition of the French, Spanish, Mexican, and Indian territories. Even if no immigrants had reached our shores since the formation of the United States, our country would still be far from having a homogeneous Anglo-Saxon population. Just the contrary is the fact. About thirty-eight million immigrants have landed here since 1820. Then we must add to this conglomeration of nationalities the twelve mil-

[38] Pearl Buck, *What America Means to Me* (New York: The John Day Company, 1943).

[39] Joseph S. Roucek, "Future Steps in Cultural Pluralism," *Journal of Educational Sociology,* XII (April, 1939), pp. 499–504.

lion Negroes, who have no Anglo-Saxon or European background and who are of an entirely different derivation. Obviously, our history must really show how the original Anglo-American culture has been modified by the continued impact of the cultures of the minority groups, conditioned, in turn, by the geographical and social factors in America and by the distance of this country from the original habitat of the immigrants. More and more researches are and will be available on the role played by these minorities in American life, prepared especially by the descendants from these minority groups able to read the languages of the smaller and less known nations. Furthermore, little effort has been made to popularize their findings and to incorporate them in our textbooks. This applies especially to our national minorities known as "new" immigrants. It is seldom known, in spite of the considerable documentary evidence, that most of the so-called "new" immigrant groups date their first arrivals from pre-Revolutionary days.

All these groups have brought with them their folkways, legends, folklore, and folk tales. But hardly anything has been done to preserve, classify, and describe these marginal cultures which are inextricably interwoven with our American history. Yet, here we have a culture common to all peoples, the knowledge of which can go a long way in overriding national animosities. In spite of the superabundance of this material, our American institutions have not even begun to develop systematically and on a long-range basis such archival, library, and museum collections, although such treasures may be had today for the mere asking, and may not be available tomorrow simply because they are disappearing and are being destroyed in proportion as the older generations are dying out and the succeeding generations are "Americanizing" themselves. We need to preserve the immigrant books, pamphlets, files of newspapers and magazines, reports of immigrant societies and organizations of any kind, portraits of minority pioneers and eminent persons, photographs and pictures illustrating their life in America, autographs and manuscripts, maps, medals, badges, etc. No comprehensive understanding of the United States can be acquired without a thorough acquaintance with the past and present conditions of all our racial and national minorities, based on a patient research in such documents, now scattered and abandoned in "national homes," churches, and attics and cellars of private homes.

The dissemination of such knowledge would help a lot to promote internationalism "right at home," where our idealism can be put to a practical test. When interested, for instance, in advancing our knowledge of Poles, why not secure permanent and temporary exhibits of arts, crafts, and literature, hold group conferences, present pageants, drama, music recitals and dance festivals of Poland in cooperation with our American Poles and their descendants? By drafting them, as well as all others, we shall be able to identify and preserve the cultural contributions of our Americans of varied backgrounds for the enjoyment and pride of these groups and for the enrichment of Americans in general.

It is true that here and there much has been done in the way of experimentation, but most of it has been limited to the presentation of such programs to the Poles and the Americans interested in Poland, the Czechs and Americans interested in Czechoslovakia, and so on. In the future, what will have to be emphasized more is that the American democratic way of life demands the creation of an intelligent consciousness of our national group life and our relationships to the rest of the world. Concretely speaking, our intercultural education will have to make *all* Americans and *all* our minorities aware of the values of *all* other cultures on the assumption that no one culture contains all favorable elements, but that each group has a share in building our democracy.

In line with this thought, the school specifically must take the lead in bringing about a greater appreciation of our minority cultures. Only through the adoption of a conscious program by all agencies of education will it be possible to avoid here the horrible tendencies in the racial, national, and religious strife now taking place abroad—and at home. Additional concrete suggestions are: further development of adult education among foreign-born parents, with special emphasis on the elimination of culture conflicts of their children; the use of English in introducing foreign-language radio programs; the rapid development of English periodicals, containing sections in foreign languages, promoting the decrease of foreign habits, and emphasizing less the affairs of the homelands and more the national problems of the United States; and the preparation of films portraying the contributions of national groups in America.

Ultimately, however, all aspects of intercultural education will have to become an accepted part of general education, without the continued requirement of special approaches, materials, and techniques.

LIMITS ON CULTURAL PLURALISM

We must not, however, oversentimentalize the possible solutions. It ought to be remembered that it is not only necessary to secure legal guarantees for all minorities, but also to establish the position that the rule of the majority is no crime in a democracy or in any other form of government. If anything has been taught to us by Hitler's psychological warfare, it is the principle that there are limits to the possible demands of any minority, especially when the rights of minorities are utilized for political purposes dangerous to the interests of the United States and its democratic way of life.[40] Even those who used to prefer foreign problems to domestic ones to worry about have learned since Pearl Harbor that one form of our culture conflicts, that growing from the existence of our racial and national minorities, was intensified by the influence of the propaganda emanating from aggressive foreign dictatorships, which were trying to attract a large group of our foreign-born inhabitants and their American-born children to ideologies quite alien to our ways of thinking; although the duty of these citizens was, and always will be, unquestionably, to render primary allegiance to the United States and not to the rulers of these foreign states. Several minorities of the United States can help to solve this aspect of America's problem by refusing to be exploited by their so-called fatherlands for political

[40] Cf. Joseph S. Roucek, "Editorial," *Journal of Educational Sociology*, XII, 8 (April, 1939), pp. 449–450; Roucek, "Fifth Column, The Strategy of Treachery, and Total Espionage," chapter 25, pp. 714, 742, and "International Movements and Secret Organizations as Instruments of Power Politics," chapter 26, pp. 743–762, in Thorsten V. Kalijarvi, *Modern World Politics* (New York: Thomas Y. Crowell, 1942); Roucek, "Foreign Politics and Our Minorities," *Phylon*, II, 1 (1941), pp. 41–56; Roucek, "Sabotage and America's Minorities," *World Affairs Interpreter*, XIV (April, 1943), pp. 45–66.

purposes. Furthermore, all of us should remember that it will be necessary to prevent a minority within a minority from exercising a veto power over the destiny of the majority.

The problem of group discrimination has by no means been solved and will cost us much in the future in maladjustment, in crime, social and political conflicts, and disorganization. Many steps will have to be taken in the near future in order to make the theory of the intercultural education more effective.[41] Ultimately, however, all aspects of intercultural education will have to become an accepted part of general education.

BIBLIOGRAPHY

Adamic, Louis, *From Many Lands* (New York: Harper & Brothers, 1940). A standard popular introduction to this field.

Bell, Reginald, *Public School Education of Second-Generation Japanese in California* (Stanford University, Cal.: Stanford University Press, 1935).

Bowers, D. F., Ed., *Foreign Influences in American Life* (Princeton: Princeton University Press, 1944). A discussion of the direct influence which the immigrant and his culture have had on American life since colonial days. Weak on the influences of the Central-Eastern immigrant.

Brown, Francis J. & Roucek, Joseph S., Eds., *One America: Our Racial and National Minorities* (New York: Prentice-Hall, 1945). Deals with all the "new" immigrant groups and their influence on American life.

Cassidy, Florence G., *Second-Generation Youth* (New York: The Women's Press, 1930).

Haiman, Mierzyslaw, *Problems of Polish American History Writing* (reprinted from *The Quarterly Bulletin of the Polish Institute of Arts and Sciences in America,* January, 1943).

Jasinski, W. J., *On the Assimilation of the Poles in America* (Orchard Lake, Mich.: Dabrowski Foundation of the Polish Seminary, 1941).

Lewis, Read, "Immigrants and Their Children," *Social Work Year Book* (1935).

[41] Cf. Joseph S. Roucek, "Future Steps in Cultural Pluralism," *Journal of Educational Sociology,* XII, 8 (April, 1939), pp. 499–507. William E. Vickery and Stewart G. Cole, *Intercultural Education in American Schools* (New York: Harper, 1942), is the best theoretical approach to this problem.

Mariano, J. H., *The Second Generation of Italians in New York City* (Boston: Christopher Publishing House, 1921).

Murra, W. F., "Improving Inter-Group Relationships in American Life," *The Civic Leader,* XXVIII (May 1, 1944), pp. 1–3; "Notes on Teaching Inter-Group Relations," *Ibid.,* XXXVIII (Dec. 4, 1944), pp. 1–13.

Roucek, Joseph S., Ed., "Culture Conflicts and Education," *Journal of Educational Sociology,* XII (April, 1939); *Misapprehensions about Central-Eastern Europe in Anglo-Saxon Historiography* (reprinted from *The Quarterly Bulletin of the Polish Institute of Arts and Sciences in America,* January, 1944).

Sherman, Mandel, *Mental Conflicts and Personality* (New York: Longmans, Green, 1938), Chapter III, "Culture Conflicts," pp. 88–128.

Smith, W. C., *The Second-Generation Oriental in America* (Honolulu: University of Hawaii, 1927).

Strong, Edward K., *The Second-Generation Japanese Problem* (Stanford University Press, Cal., 1934).

White House Conference on Child Health and Protection, *The Delinquent Child* (New York: D. Appleton-Century, 1932), Section IVC2.

V

GROUPS AND EDUCATIONAL OPPORTUNITY

BY

EDMUND DE S. BRUNNER PH.D.

Professor in Rural Education, Teachers College, Columbia University

The fascinating and sometimes baffling phenomena of group life, which are being explored in this series, have, as the very outline shows, numerous manifestations. The definitions and theoretical considerations clustering around the group concept have been dealt with adequately by my predecessors. We are now in that part of the series which deals with the manifestation or illustration of these theories within some of the important areas of our social life. Today our area of interest is education.

Yet it is also true that within any such large area many groups are self-selective. They can be defined by the way in which they operate. Separate groups form within a large area of interest. On matters of more or less universal importance to those concerned with the area they may unite in a large aggregate. In other lesser matters there may be sharp differences of opinion and behavior. Thus in the depths of the agricultural depression there was practical unanimity of opinion among all farmers and all subgroups of farmers with reference to certain policies generally lumped under the term "farm relief." By their recorded votes farmers approved the provisions of the first Agricultural Adjustment Act by more than fifty to one. But today there are sharp differences among the subgroups that make up the totality of the farmers of the country. The American Farm Bureau Federation stands for certain policies which the Farmers Union deems antisocial. The commercial farmers of the south are opposed to the programs designed to improve the lot of the low-income clients of the Farm Security Administration. And so on.

Moreover, it is quite possible, when the sociologist looks at masses of data out of which he seeks to bring order and extract meaning, that he will discover measurable likenesses of behavior and of conditions pertaining to the population of definable areas or even small localities. To such population aggregates the term "group" is at times applied. For the purposes of our discussion today I shall include this latter consideration because of its importance with respect not only to the general area of education but also to the welfare of our nation.

To some it may seem desirable that I should pause at this point to define education. But it is an institution, in the large sense of the term, so complex in its structure, so manifold in its expressions, so many-sided, that there would be no time for my main theme, should I embark upon such an enterprise. Obviously the education of youth, which includes in large measure their schooling, must be a prominent element in today's discussion, as must certain aspects of adult education. Instead, then, of meticulous definition I shall rather attempt merely to make clear at each step what it is in education that I am considering.

First of all, it is important to take note of the educational efforts of certain well-recognized groups in our society. It is important because ours is a democratic society. Our children are not all poured through the same mold at the behest of the state. True, we support an elaborate system of education at public expense but it is not a Federal system. Rather we have forty-eight educational systems. Our public schools differ in curriculum, in amount and methods of support, in certification requirements of teachers, and so on. Even within the states there is wide variation in the conduct of the educational enterprise. This state of affairs is responsible for some of the most serious of our educational problems, from the point of view of national welfare and of social groups. On the other hand, it is also responsible for many of the advances in education, in the efforts to shape the curriculum to meet the varying needs of states and regions, influenced as these needs are by varying conditions both social and economic. It is fundamental in our thinking of democracy that education be a local function.

We have carried this idea further. Side by side with tax-supported schools, colleges, and universities we permit private institutions of the same academic rank.

One to two centuries ago it was not deemed to be necessary to give education to all children. It was a prerogative of those from the advantaged families; especially was this true in the South. Thus many so-called private schools grew up, something in the tradition of Eton, Rugby, and the so-called public schools of England. Many of them were and are so-called military schools. The students were drawn from particular strata of the population. They went on to college in the average case. Instruction, and the school life even more, reinforced the mores of the dominant if not the ruling group in the society, even though its rule was tempered by votes of the whole citizenry.

It cannot be denied that some at least of the motivations for sending children to such institutions are today only secondarily, or to put it more tactfully, only partly educational. Attendance means acquaintance with "the right people" and graduation a passport to levels of social life not reached by the many. It takes very little to arouse criticism with respect to the undemocratic character of such an arrangement. In a nearby suburb some ten years ago an effort was made by some citizens to reduce the public-school system's budget. The fact that some of the leaders of this attempt sent their own children to expensive private schools was a telling argument on the part of those who opposed the economy move. The same thing has recently reappeared on the national scene. Senator Taft of Ohio is generally credited with the defeat of the bill to extend Federal aid to public schools. In the course of the debate he named $1,200 as an ample salary for school teachers in many parts of his state. Critics of his position and of his estimate of the value of the services of public-school teachers have been quick to point out that Senator Taft's four sons learned their three "R's" at an exclusive eastern private school, where tuition costs more than $1,200 a year.

The private schools, of course, claim two contributions they deem of great social value. In the first place, they can experiment not merely in educational methods and techniques but also in offering and developing new educational services, of which guidance is an illustration. Such experimentation is less open to the tax-supported schools with their far larger enrollments, but once an experiment proves worth while it can be introduced into the public schools.

Again, the private schools assume that they train for leadership and point to the crying need of this quality in a democracy. They aver that the public schools can only raise the level of mediocrity. This is an assumption the psychologists, so far as I know, have not yet proved, for the private-school child often starts life with advantages not possessed by others. But the attitude is there. Within the year a member of the British Cabinet said to a friend of mine, "If a study were made, it would show that in every pinch where split-second thinking is needed, the aviator who wears a school tie comes through better than the one who doesn't." Well, I wish the study could be made and that it would include our own airmen.

Strictly speaking, of course, such private schools represent a socio-economic strata of society rather than a social group, but in considering the pros and cons of groups and educational advantage it is worth while to raise the issues which cluster around this phase of education in our society.

Another whole phase of private education falls much more clearly into the concept of the group. I refer to those schools which are religiously motivated and operated.

Religious sects have felt that public education fails to stress adequately the spiritual values in life. They have attempted therefore to give the necessary educational content that will fit a child for life in American society within a context that emphasizes these values. They aver that while the public school talks about character education, the parochial school does it. It is their belief that character can be built safely only on a foundation of religion. Many of them go further and provide for specific religious indoctrination within the curriculum. This education is often carried on at high cost to the participating families. They are not economically advantaged on the average. They pay their share of the support of public education and support their own schools in addition. This is a tribute to the sincerity of their convictions.

It should be pointed out that the conservation of religious ideals in our society is an abiding problem. It is clear that if the assumptions be granted, the permeation of the whole of society by such ideals would be to society's advantage. Moreover, in this country even the forty-five per cent of the population who are not aligned with institutionalized religion have come under the influence of the Judaeo-Christian tradition. It is basic in the structure of our present mores, with all allowance for the wide deviations both in the interpretation of that tradition and in the behavior patterns of individuals and religious groups within our culture.

But the diversity of our attempts to achieve religious indoctrination and the acceptance of religious values, through church-school religious education, released time, and so on, shows that society and even the religonists within it have come to no consensus as to the methods of insuring the passing on of the spiritual aspects of individual and collective living. By the same token, then, society has not wholly approved the device of the private parochial school as a means to that end. However, since this is to a considerable degree a democratic society committed to freedom of worship, it tolerates, indeed legally permits, socioreligious groups to operate their own educational institutions. Moreover, if such group-controlled schools meet the standards, it accredits them even while there is debate, largely academic, as to whether such procedures make for either social or educational advantage.

The concept of educational advantage can be much more clearly illustrated and perhaps understood when one deals not with organized social groups which operate educational institutions but rather with groups as determined by the criteria of the sociologist. These can be examined from the dual point of view of educational and social advantage.

There are many such groups. Complete answers to the issues raised by our theme today can come perhaps only from many intensive case studies. But in terms of large groups in our society data of real importance exist as a result of the 1940 Federal census. These data for the first time in our history give us information about the educational status of the population twenty-five years of age and over. There will shortly be available comparable information, including the facts with respect to school attendance of the population concerned, for those under twenty-five.

An examination of the data on the educational status of those twenty-five and over shows that for important groups in the population the democratic ideal of equality of opportunity has fallen far short of accomplishment. Within my time it is impossible to give complete documentation of this generalization but the trend of the data can be indicated by a few illustrations employing the census measurement of median years of schooling completed. This for the population of our cities is 9.6 years. For villagers it is one year less and for the farm population only eight years. Moreover, for much of the farm population, we know from Office of Education studies that the school years given averaged a month less than those completed by urban adults. Clearly we have placed our farm group at a handicap with respect to educational advantage. What that means to the cities of America, indeed to the nation, I shall show in a moment.

First, however, I wish to discuss the data a bit further. When one examines this new information on a regional or state basis it is quite clear that the far western states, especially in the cities, lead all others. It is also clear that the southern states, except for the few cities of a few states, are the lowest in the nation. More than five years separates the median urban adult in the leading region of the United States from the median farm adult in the lowest southern region. And yet let us remember that in proportion to its wealth the South spends more on education than any other region or state. It maintains, of course, a dual system of education because of the Negro.

Comparably for the nation as a whole, the educational status of the foreign-born is, depending on residence, from one to two and one fourth years below that of the native-born whites. The Negroes, who of course are native-born, are from three to four years behind. Indeed the median educational status of the Negro adult farm population is 4.1 years, only one tenth of one year above the point at which there is functional illiteracy according to the Army definition.

This sort of thing shows up even within small areas like counties or townships. In my home county one fourth of our considerable farm population is functionally illiterate. These people are of Portuguese nationality, largely from the Cape Verde and Azores Islands. They are a distinct, locally recognized social group. They are efficient farmers. It happens that our two chief crops are highly specialized and also that they are particularly valuable to the armed services. You can imagine some of the problems that arose this summer in working with these people on matters of farm labor and the deferment of farm boys and, even more, with respect to the use and procurement of fertilizer, machinery, and gas, all requiring the filling out of forms.

Let me contrast two counties I know in the same state, both rural. One has barely average soil, a hilly topography, and is settled by persons who migrated, either they themselves or their forebears two or three generations back, from the Kentucky hills. The other, one hundred miles away, has some of the best soil in the state. The predominant racial strain represented is English, the religious tradition Methodist. In both counties the cultural heritage is stamped indelibly on the social structure. In the first, the median years of schooling of the adult farm population in 1940 was 7.1, in the latter 9.0. The latter county had four times as many high-school graduates and four and one third times as many with college training as the former. Think what this means in terms of the calibre of the potential leadership of local government, school and church boards, and other social organizations. Basically of the same stock these social groups were widely different in terms of educational advantage.

The implications of these varying degrees of such educational advantage for the general or social welfare are of considerable importance.

The most obvious of these has been made familiar by the draft records of the Selective Service Administration. Not to burden you with statistics, what has happened may be summarized as follows: The highest proportions of rejectees have come from the areas where we have our greatest potential supply of manpower of military age.

These areas are also the ones where the educational status is lowest, where schools are poorest, where the economic basis of the society is weakest and where social utilities other than the school are almost nonexistent. These areas are also the ones which in the depression of the 1930's were known to the relief administrators as the Six Problem Areas. The rejections were on grounds of illiteracy and health. The health conditions reflected in large part poor nutritional practices, which, though partly the result of the economic status of the families of the rejectees, are partly remediable by adequate education, as Professor Harold Clark's experimental project in the mountains of Kentucky is showing.

The result in these areas has been a calling to the colors, even though of necessity the Army has begun taking functional illiterates, whom it requires more time to train, of a disproportionate number of the socially, educationally, and economically advantaged youth in these sections. From precisely the areas where we most need to conserve what potentially superior leadership we have, we have had to be most prodigal in the expenditure of our seed corn, so to speak. Even assuming equal loss ratios among the men of all groups and regions, the war will therefore leave our neediest areas and groups more needy relative to the rest of the nation than before the conflict. In the difficult postwar period they will be further disadvantaged. This is the price we as a nation must pay for our neglect of the democratic principle of equality of educational opportunity and advantage for all groups and regions.

But the implications are even more fundamental. Educators and sociologists have long seen them, even though the United States Senate does not yet understand them. These implications are wrapped up in our demographic situation, especially from two points of view; namely, birth rates and migration.

The birth rates of the United States were declining from 1935 to 1940. We as a nation were not producing enough babies to insure even a stationary population. The cities of America were raising only three fourths enough children, but the national deficit was only four per cent. Obviously, the rural population made up the difference. I have already shown that the educational status of the rural group is at a disadvantage compared to the urban in most regions of the nation.

In some of the more rural states, such as Mississippi, there are twice as many children of school age in each 1,000 of the population as in New York and California. Even if there were equal per capita wealth, which is far from the case, it would cost twice as much per adult in Mississippi as in New York or California to effect equality of educational opportunity. Correcting for wealth differences, the discrepancy is between four- and fivefold.

This is bad enough in a democracy but it is not all. Technological advances in agriculture, which, measured by production per worker, have been almost as great in the last seventy-five years as the advances in industry, compel these rural youth to migrate. During the 1930's there were 250 farm youth for every 100 farms that became available through the death or retirement of the operator. Surplus rural youth then go cityward. They have been reared and educated in the country. They contribute their strength and ability to the city. This is an economic gift of rural to urban America which in peace times is the equivalent of from one tenth to one fifth of the net income of American farmers. But the youth of this group have not had the educational advantage available in our cities.

The city is careful indeed of the sources of its milk, food, and water supplies. It is careless in the extreme with respect to the source of its human supply that compensates for its own deficient birth rate.

It is on these facts that the social and economic arguments for Federal aid to education rest. If you are opposed to such a policy, well and good, but then it is incumbent upon you to help solve the problems inherent in our neglect of equality of educational advantage for all groups.

May I give you a single illustration of how this operates, one of which I have from firsthand knowledge. In a certain middlewestern city in 1937 the leading department store noticed that in three wards its sales had fallen off very rapidly both in dollar value and in quality of goods. There were some angry words at the board meeting and suggestions of dismissing personnel, but the personnel manager himself asked time to investigate. This is what he found. Into these wards in the three preceding years and partly as a result of relief policies there had come thousands of families from some of the more disadvantaged sections of a nearby southern state. In these three wards the crime rate in this period, proportionate to the population, had almost doubled. The juvenile delinquency rate had gone up one hundred and thirty per cent. The number of fires had increased eighty per cent. The load of the social case workers for causes other than poverty and relief had increased fifty per cent. The average age of the children in the schools had increased one year for each grade. That city is paying a heavy cost for its increased population, a cost measureable in dollars and cents and in social losses. These people were not criminals. Their forebears were not among the finest stock that ever migrated to these shores in colonial days, but they had become mired on the poor soil of their beautiful foothills in the Appalachians. They had been neglected socially and educationally. They were unable to adjust to the modern industrial era which had passed them by but into which they had suddenly been plunged. The city was paying the price of the neglect of the democratic principle of the necessity of equality of educational advantage for all groups.

It was early recognized by the founding fathers that democracy depended upon the education of the masses, who are, in the last analysis, the government. The high correlation between the presence of racial and religious prejudice in some groups and the absence of educational advantage in these same groups shows that in this, as in so much else, our fathers were supremely wise, but we have neglected their wisdom. The fate of our democracy lies in the balance on the field of battle, and we face that test in high confidence. But in the decades that stretch ahead, in the postwar era in which the hopes and fears of all the years of our unfolding social processes are met, our fate is also in the balance. And to insure that what we hope becomes fact and what we fear is banished, we must highly and perhaps first resolve that the educational inequalities among groups, races, and regions shall, along with Hitler and Tojo, be done away with and the concept of educational advantage for the sake of the general welfare shall become an accepted policy of this most powerful of the democracies.

BIBLIOGRAPHY

Norton, John K. and Lawler, Eugene S., *An Inventory of Public School Expenditures in the United States*. Two volumes, mimeographed.

Edwards, Newton, *Equal Educational Opportunity for Youth*, American Council on Education (Washington, 1939).

National Resources Planning Board, *Problems of a Changing Population* (Washington, 1938).

VI

EDUCATION AND GROUP ADVANTAGE

BY

I. L. KANDEL, PH.D.

Professor of Education, Teachers College, Columbia University

The chief characteristic of American education, when compared with the educational systems in most other countries of the world, has always been the ideal of providing equality of opportunity for all. For the past twenty-five years serious doubts have arisen whether this ideal is actually effective in practice. Since this aspect of the problem has already been presented in a previous lecture, it is unnecessary to discuss in detail the fact that, under the present system of administration and financial support of education, opportunities for education are in practice not equally distributed throughout the country. The wealth of the country is unevenly distributed; the poorest states have larger numbers of children to educate; there are differences in ability to support an adequate system of education between the states and, in each state, between urban areas and between urban and rural communities.

From this point of view the accessibility of educational opportunities is dependent largely upon accident of residence. The number of days in which schools are open each year, the administration of compulsory-attendance laws, the availability of primary schools equipped to meet the demands of modern education, adequate provision of different types of secondary education adapted to the varied abilities of pupils, and the needs of the local community, accessibility of opportunities for education beyond the high school, and the preparation, quality, and remuneration of teachers, and the amount of money available for the support of schools—all these aspects which enter into the provision of equality of educational opportunities are dependent upon the place where a child happens to be living. It is for these reasons that the movement has developed in the past quarter of a century to secure national co-operation in the form of increased Federal aid for education. During this war, as in the last, evidence of the unequal distribution of education has again been accumulated. Enough draftees to make several battalions were rejected on account of illiteracy and physical defects, while thousands of others who had acquired the rudiments of reading and writing were functionally illiterate in the sense that they could not understand written directions. At the upper end of the educational ladder serious deficiencies were found in knowledge in mathematics, sciences, and foreign languages.

All these facts point to the inadequate provision of educational opportunities both in quantity and in quality and indicate that accessibility of adequate facilities for education are dependent upon the accident of residence. There is, however, another aspect of the problem of education and group advantage which is just as serious, and that is the fact that the amount of education which is open to American youth is dependent upon the accident of socioeconomic conditions. In other words, there is ample evidence to prove that there is a close relationship between parental income and economic status and the amount of education enjoyed by boys and girls in the country. The issue, therefore, is whether the country is making adequate use of its human resources and insuring, through the system of education, that each individual is given the best opportunity to make the most of his potential abilities. From the point of view of the individual the question is whether opportunities are available for him to acquire such education and training as will make the highest contribution to society of which he is capable. From the social point of view the question is whether society is providing the right kind of education for the right individual under the right teacher in order to secure the best returns in accordance with its own needs.

The issue has been widely discussed in professional journals for the past twenty years but has not, to the best of my knowledge, been adequately brought to the attention of the public. The notion seems to be widespread that the needs of all groups are met by the provision of free education at public expense. The absence of tuition fees, however, does not equalize the opportunities for education for all. The cost of books and school supplies in some parts of the country, the expenses for incidentals in connection, particularly, with extracurricular activities, the increasing cost of maintenance in board, food, and clothing of growing youth, and the sacrifice of such financial contributions as youth could make to the home—all these factors tend to militate against the fullest distribution of educational opportunities. Although the evidence on the subject is equivocal, it is not clear that the practice of working for an education, which is uniquely characteristic of the United States, does not detract from the fullest enjoyment of equality of educational opportunities.

The whole subject of education and group advantage was opened up by Dr. George S. Counts in 1922 when he published a study on *The Selective Character of Secondary Education*. On the basis of a study of 17,992 cases (8,222 boys and 9,770 girls) in four cities in different parts of the country Dr. Counts found that the selective principle still existed in the American high schools in 1922. There was at that time a close relationship between parental occupations and, therefore, of parental income and the enjoyment of the privileges of secondary education. Both attendance and persistence in high schools paralleled the economic and occupational status of parents; the largest number of pupils attending and continuing in high schools through the four years of the course came from five nonlabor groups—professional, managerial, commercial, clerical, and proprietary; the poorest representation was from the lower grades of common labor, personal service, miners, lumberworkers, fishermen, miscellaneous trades and machine operatives; the intermediate group was made up of children from parents engaged in printing, building, and machine trades and public and transportation services. Dr. Counts's study proved conclusively that the enjoyment of educational opportunities was determined by the socioeconomic status of parental occupations, their educational and intellectual status, and the stability of employment. These factors also affected the choice of courses in high schools; boys and girls from the lower occupational groups tended to elect practical courses which provided a quick preparation for wage-earning careers—a tendency which meant that the children of the laboring classes were destined to follow in the footsteps of their fathers. Dr. Counts also found a relationship between attendance at high schools and the size of families, although this did not appear to him to be a determining factor. Finally, the study showed that children of native parents attend the high school in larger numbers than children of immigrant parents and that more children of immigrants from Northern Europe are found in high schools than children of immigrants from Southern and Eastern Europe; thus the number of children of Russian Jews in the high schools was about equal to the number of children of native parents, and these were followed by children of Irish, German, and British parents. Of the children of immigrants boys were more likely than girls to choose a college-preparatory course. In 1922, then, the high schools were attended more largely by children of the well-to-do classes, and not only was their number larger but more of them were likely to graduate than children of other socioeconomic groups.

Since 1922, the situation at the high-school level has changed but only because the age of compulsory school attendance has been raised in many states to sixteen, seventeen, and eighteen. Nevertheless, although the enrollments in high schools have increased from 2,494,676 in 1920 to somewhat over 7,000,000 in 1940, nearly 2,000,000 youth of high-school age were not in school. The reasons have been stated in a report (1943) published by the National Resources Planning Board and they are as follows:

(1) The labor of children is either needed at home or their earnings are needed to supplement family incomes. (2) Parents are unable to buy clothes and school supplies and provide funds for incidental expenses.

Although enrollments in high schools continued to increase in the past twenty years, the conditions revealed by Counts did not change. Thus the National Survey of Secondary Education, published in

1932, showed that 31 per cent of the students left school for economic reasons; in Maryland the American Youth Commission found that the percentage leaving because of lack of funds was even higher—54 per cent; financial causes for leaving school were among the most important found by the Regents' Inquiry in New York State. High-school authorities have for a long time been aware of the fact that large numbers of pupils drop out because they find the work too difficult, but efforts have in many places been made to adapt the curriculum to the abilities, needs, and interests of the pupils. Those who still drop out, despite these efforts, are recognized to be inferior in ability. There are, however, many of high ability who leave school because of economic necessity.

As the enrollments in high schools increased, partly as a result of the raising of the age of compulsory attendance and partly because of the diminishing opportunities for employment, attention has gradually shifted to the next stage on the educational ladder. More recently a number of studies have appeared on the extent to which students avail themselves of the opportunity to continue their education beyond the high school. The result of all the studies is that more than half of the high-school graduates fail to go on to college or some equivalent institution and that the reason is, in the main, economic.

Of these studies one of the most interesting is on "The Relation of Parental Income to College Opportunity" by Miss H. B. Goetsch (*School Review,* January, 1940, pp. 26 ff.). Miss Goetsch made a study of 1,023 students who had graduated from twelve Milwaukee high schools. Only 35 per cent of the capable students were in full-time attendance in some college; 4 per cent were in part-time attendance; 19 per cent were enrolled in some post-high-school institution; 42 per cent were not in any school at all. In other words, more than half of the students capable of profiting thereby were not in college. The most common reason for this was economic—either lack of finances or pressure to work at home or add to the family income. There was obviously a close relation between attendance at college and parental income. The median parental earnings of those who attended college full-time were $1,988.46; of those who attended some other institution full-time the parental earnings were $1,894.58; where the earnings were $1,300, attendance at school was part-time; and where they were $1,285.21, there was no chance that school would be attended at all. Educational advantages were greatest where parental earnings were highest and vice versa. The ratio of youth in college decreased as parental incomes decreased; where parental incomes were $5,000 or over, only 6 per cent of the youth were not in college, while 80 per cent were not in college where parental incomes were $500 or less. Even the choice of professional courses is determined by parental incomes and, apparently, in the following order from the highest to the lowest: (1) law; (2) medicine and dentistry; (3) liberal arts; (4) journalism; (5) engineering; (6) education; (7) commerce; (8) nursing; and (9) industrial trades. So too the length of course taken is determined by parental income, ranging from less than four years for median parental incomes of $1,416.67 to more than four years for median incomes of $2,150. Finally, a relation was found between parental income and the distance of the college attended.

It is clear from this study that the notion that the only barrier to a college education is native ability is false. Many young men and women of ability are unable to take advantage of opportunities for higher education for economic reasons. This conclusion reached in the Milwaukee study does not stand alone; it is corroborated by findings for the state of Ohio that as many good students do not continue their education beyond the high school as poor ones enter college. In Kentucky it was estimated by high-school advisers that 63 per cent of the high-school graduates with the requisite ability did not proceed to college for financial reasons. It was found further that in a predominantly rural state, relatively more urban than rural high-school graduates enrolled in college and that of rural students boys were given a chance before the ablest rural girls. The same relation between parental income and college attendance was found in Kentucky as in Milwaukee. The general conclusion for Kentucky was that about half of the best college risks graduating from the high schools of the state fail to go to college each year, while about one in seven of the poor college risks do go. The chief cause for this situation was economic.[1]

The danger to which these studies point is the gradual stratification of American youth. Rosanoff in a study of this aspect of the problem reported a strong positive correlation between the father's occupation and socioeconomic status and the occupations of sons and daughters. In other words, the father's economic position conditions to a measurable extent the economic position of youth, since the occupations which they enter correlate in turn to a considerable extent with the amount of education that they were able to enjoy. Youth from families engaged in professions, managerial occupations, or skilled trades have a distinct advantage in continuing their education and in securing employment in similar occupations. Only in the case of girls is there a tendency for them to be free from the influence of their father's occupations but they, too, tend to be limited to sales and clerical positions. In general these conditions mean that economic stratification follows parental incomes and occupations and that this stratification may become accentuated as age increases—those in professional and managerial careers will enjoy increasing incomes, while those in unskilled and semiskilled occupations will rise slowly but to a low maximum income. In this study as in the others the conclusion is inescapable that the amount of education received and, therefore, the occupations open to youth are determined by family income and status.[2]

All the studies analyzed so far and dealing with opportunities for high-school and college education confirm an earlier study by J. B. Maller on the "Economic and Social Correlatives of School Progress in New York City" (*Teachers College Record,* May, 1933, pp. 655 ff.). Dr. Maller found that even in an educational system as closely unified and integrated as that of New York City the rates of scholastic progress at the elementary level differ greatly from school to school. The rates of progress correlated with various social, economic, biological,

[1] Davis, H. L., *Utilization of Potential College Ability Found in the June, 1940, Graduates of Kentucky High Schools* (Lexington, Ky., 1942).

[2] Rosanoff, A. C., "Economic Stratification of Youth," *Journal of Educational Research,* April, 1939, pp. 592 ff.

and ethnic factors characteristic of the neighborhood in which the school was located. Neighborhoods of low economic status were low in the rate of school progress and vice versa. Neighborhoods in which the rate of school progress was above average had lower birth and death rates, lower rates of infant mortality, less juvenile delinquency, less economic dependency, and a higher average of intelligence.

A number of interesting issues which affect the welfare of individuals, groups, and society as a whole emerge from these studies. The major issue is whether society can afford to accept the conclusion of one investigator that "as far as educational opportunity is concerned, the importance of being born into the 'right' family cannot be overemphasized." It is obvious that the mere provision of free schools is not enough to equalize the educational opportunities and to extend the advantages of education to the children and youth of all groups. Inadequate provision is made to care for the health of children and youth. Conditions for a healthy physical and mental start are not equal as long as an adequate supply of nursery schools and kindergartens does not exist. At the elementary-school level insufficient attention is paid to differences in the social, economic, and intellectual backgrounds of the families from which pupils are drawn. At the high-school level there is great waste of potential ability through failure to provide financial support to pupils who are compelled to leave for economic reasons. And, finally, much still remains to be done to make it possible for able students to enter and remain in colleges and technical institutions until they complete their courses; at present less than half of those who have the ability to meet the standards of a higher education are debarred because of lack of funds. It is still an open question whether the practice of working for one's education is sound or not; although there is evidence that scholastic records are not affected by such work, students who devote much time to earning a living are inevitably deprived of some of the advantages of corporate living both in high school and in college.

Efforts to meet the situation have been made through the establishment of loan funds and scholarship aid, but the practice is neither uniform nor standardized. If society establishes and maintains schools to improve the quality of its members as citizens and as workers.

much of the money devoted to education is likely to be wasted, if those best able to profit by it are debarred from going as far as their abilities permit for financial reasons. In New York State the number of able candidates for scholarships is about ten times the number awarded each year. During the depression a precedent was established by the National Youth Administration which made it possible for the youth of families of certain income levels to remain in high school and college. The studies which have been discussed in this paper indicate that the situation which the National Youth Administration was created to meet is not a crisis condition; it is endemic. Hence if the United States is to make the most of its human resources by enabling all children and youth to receive that education for which they are best equipped by their ability in the interests of themselves and their country, then a further step in the provision of equality of educational opportunity must be taken and aid must be provided in the form of scholarships adapted in amount to family income, on the one hand, and the abilities of the students on the other.

I know of no better summary of this paper than a statement made about ten years ago by E. L. Thorndike and based on a study of the educational careers of 785 boys in New York City. On the basis of this study Dr. Thorndike came to the following conclusion which deserves to be quoted in full because it bears so closely on the subject of my paper, "Education and Group Advantage":

> Zeal to produce more schooling, that is, to increase the amount of schooling given in our country, has been one of America's fine idealisms. Such zeal should be maintained, but with it there should be equal zeal to distribute this education so that those will have most who can use it best. What evidence we now have indicates that the ablest receive very little more than the least able. For every boy in the top forty of our 785 who stayed in school beyond the age of eighteen, there were nearly ten boys below average ability who did so. The passion for equalization which had a certain nobility when a large percentage of children barely learned to read and write becomes unwise, almost ridiculous, when the question is of spending our resources to keep in school boys of sixteen, or seventeen, or eighteen who would be happier and more useful at work or at play.

Our increased resources should be used to aid young men and women whom nature and nurture have chosen to profit from schooling.

Doubtless, great ability will often manage to get education outside of schools or to get along without it, but those who can do so much for the world with so little are the very ones who should be given more. In the wars we are incessantly waging against disease, misery, depravity, injustice, and ugliness, we should not provide our best marksmen with the poorest weapons nor ask our bravest to fight with their naked hands.[3]

BIBLIOGRAPHY

Davis, H. L., *Utilization of Potential College Ability Found in the June, 1940, Graduates of Kentucky High Schools* (Lexington, Ky., 1942).

Rosanoff, A. C., "Economic Stratification of Youth," *Journal of Educational Research,* April, 1939.

"The Distribution of Education," *School Review,* Vol. XL, May, 1932.

[3] "The Distribution of Education," *School Review,* Vol. XL, May, 1932, pp. 335 ff.

VII

GROUPS AND SOCIAL STATUS

BY

ROBERT S. LYND, PH.D.

Professor of Sociology, Columbia University

I shall use "groups" here to refer both to those who consciously associate themselves, either tightly or loosely, and to those who, as a by-product of this more positive process of association by other people, are forced into an identity as a group that they might not otherwise seek to stress. That is, I want to include the processes in our culture that lead to specific voluntary associations such as Rotary, Chambers of Commerce, and Thanatopsis Clubs, as well as those that cleave off groups like "classes" and "Jews" and "Negroes" as objects of discrimination.

Both groups and social status are sifting devices used in society to sort out large populations in terms of preference and power. They are rooted in individual differences in capacity, temperament, and interest, and in the individual's need to belong and to sort himself out in relation to society. Around these needs and differences among individual persons cultural institutions have grown up that express power and likes and dislikes collectively rather than merely on the level of the single person. Whether group and status lines are socially constructive or are stiffened by offensive-defensive tactics such as color or race bars into formal structure like social castes or social classes depends upon the economic and social developments within a given culture.

A dozen people living on a South Sea island—two adult males, their wives and children, and two surviving elders—may conceivably be devoid of self-conscious grouping and assignment of status. But any large society living by even a moderately complex culture inevitably exhibits self-conscious groups and assignments of social status around one or more focal interests.

Accepting this tendency, rooted in the nature of individual and social life, to form groups and to develop status with resulting cleavages, what is the norm, *i.e.*, the desired goal, of groupings and assignments of status that a democratic society in 1943 should aim at? I say "should" because I regard life as purposive, experimental, and constantly in the making. And I regard institutions as malleable instruments for helping men to do what they want to do.

In regard to groups, the norm should be that kind of sorting out of individuals that (a) facilitates personal growth by encouraging significantly like persons to live with and receive stimulus from like, and that (b) encourages the groups so formed to find their places with and to co-operate with all other groups in the society within a positive structure of common social goals emphasizing common objectives and growth for the whole society and the necessary contribution of each special group to the common endeavor.

In regard to social status, the norm should be that the entire hierarchy of status be open to all, depending solely upon capacity and willingness to contribute to the whole society's objectives, with no tolerance at all of the right of any group to confer special status upon itself and to restrict or close access to such status for reasons other than capacity and willingness to serve the whole society's objectives.

Now let us take these two norms for social grouping and for assignment of status within society and use them as a yardstick to appraise the adequacy of what we have today in the cultural system in which you and I live.

1. Taking our network of groups first, do we Americans have a positive policy of facilitating association? The answer is, obviously, "No." Instead, we impute rationality and freedom to the individual and assume he will find his way. No student of group association in American life can view the resulting restless melange with satisfaction. Millions of Americans, especially those living in cities, fail of finding any group life at all worthy of that name. A marked characteristic of the groups we *do* join is their transitoriness, or, if not

transitory, their lack of spontaneity. By transitoriness I refer to the restlessness and instability so characteristic of group life in the United States. By lack of spontaniety I refer to the tendency to formality and monotony in these groups.

Far too little attention is given to the basic quality of aloneness in liberal individualistic society. At the top of the social scale, as a recent advertisement said: "No one has time to get acquainted any more. People are introduced in mumbles, meet in snatches, and disappear." This is, of course, an exaggeration, but I want to express the tendency. The advertisement went on to suggest an expensive perfume as a social solvent. Down the income scale, where people can't employ expensive possessions "to make friends and influence people," people cling to socializing institutions like the "pub" in England. A recent note cited the fact that people are drifting back from the model garden cities to the slums of the East End of London because the new housing estates lack "pubs."

We Americans are called "a nation of joiners," but our rates of joining are notably uneven. It is the upper middle and upper classes in Middletown who complain that they "belong to too many things," while the working class includes relatively more of the socially lost—the un-grouped. A 1940 study of Franklin, Indiana (population 5,700), reveals that at income levels under $100 a month one quarter of all the men and one fifth of the women have no organizational ties at all, *i.e.,* church, lodge, patriotic, as well as political and recreational clubs of all kinds including even neighborhood card clubs. But at income levels of $100 and over, only three per cent of the men and four per cent of the women have no organizational ties. Combining the figures for adult males and females, only 13 per cent of Franklin's adult population with incomes of under $100 a month belong to more than two types of organization; while, of those with incomes of $100 a month and over, 44 per cent belong to more than two types.[1] The Bureau of Labor Statistics income and expenditure studies for 1935-36, covering an unusually adequate cross section of the entire American population, reveal that "Club dues (including

[1] W. G. Mather, "Income and Social Participation," *American Sociological Review,* June 1941.

all social and recreational clubs, but omitting trade-unions, professional societies, and business organizations) show a greater change with income than any other item of recreational expense." For fourteen middle-sized cities (population 35–70,000) distributed over all parts of the country, total family social and recreational club dues averaged under $1.00 a year on all income levels under $1,000; rose to $5.20 at the $2,250–2,499 level; to $10.90 at $2,500–2,999; $19.90 at $3,000–3,499; and to $38.60 at $5,000 and over. The same source affords eloquent evidence of differences in "joining" in different cities and in cities of different sizes. At income level $1,750–1,999, Chicago and New York families average $1.90 and $2.40, respectively, per year for social and recreational club dues, while the fourteen middle-sized cities averaged $4.80, and nine small cities (population 10–20,000) averaged $4.60.[2] While social and recreational clubs requiring the payment of dues do not exhaust all the possibilities of belonging to leisure-time social groups, these figures suggest not only that belonging tends to depend upon income but also that large cities tend to have a lower average of belonging to organized groups than do cities of well under 100,000. From the point of view of human need, one might reasonably expect both of these tendencies to be reversed, for both with poverty and the anonymity of large cities the need of secure ties to one's fellows presumably increases. It looks as though ours is a culture far from encouraging association according to any rational appraisal of human need. Rather, groups and cleavages are simply allowed to happen casually.

When we face the part of our norm for democratic grouping that concerns "the significantly like," the American social scene is no less unsatisfactory than we have just seen it to be as regards the sheer numerical aspect of belonging. The overwhelmingly dominant criterion of significant likeness in our culture is likeness in wealth. Nearly all the subtleties of human likeness and difference are played down. *Similes cum similibus* largely means with us similar achievement of, or life chances to achieve, money. In passing, it is

[2] *Family Expenditures in Selected Cities,* 1935–36, Vol. VII, "Recreation, Reading, Formal Education, Tobacco, Contributions and Personal Taxes." Bulletin 648. Government Printing Office, 1941, pp. 41, 43.

significant that the one mandatory social tie in American society is the tie to a regular pay check. Beyond that, one needs to belong to nobody and to nothing. One can buy everything else impersonally without assuming reciprocal responsibility as a member of any enduring group. Not alone as regards food, clothing, and shelter, but even in leisure one may to a large extent buy one's way, as, for example, one sits among massed rows of anonymity at the movies. We have gone a long way toward making the "American way" an impersonal way. We have, especially in our larger cities, contrived a way for losing people in crowds.[3] In such a social environment, so reckless of the subtleties of human association, the more genuinely significant likenesses among persons tend to be ridden over and exploited instrumentally in the effort to achieve money likeness. In an unpublished paper Otto Kirchheimer uses the expression, "the racket stage of social organization," to characterize the present. By this he means a social system in which both joining and the aims of organizations are not free and spontaneous but controlled by the need to muscle in on an apparatus of power which controls life chances in the culture.

Look around you in your own community. Watch newcomers in the community exploit membership in the socially correct church in order to get to know the "right" people. I am sure you have no illusions that such "rightness" refers to genuine qualitative subtleties. Watch "literary" clubs turn into social clubs with papers on the Parthenon and "Our Latin-American Neighbors" hung uneasily on them like a frieze.

Here, in discussing dominance of money-making in our social sorting, let me anticipate my discussion of status to point out two things: first, the current blurring of status in terms of the job, and, second, the stress on indicating the amount of money one earns by

[3] Cf. in this connection Robert M. Coates's novel, *Yesterday's Burdens,* published ten years ago. The author reverses the usual fiction technique of letting the central figure grow on one as the story progresses. Instead, he takes his promising young hero to the city and there loses him as thoroughly as possible. As the author remarks, ". . . instead of seeking to individualize him and pin him down to a story, [the book proceeds] to generalize more and more about him—to let him become like the figures in a crowd, and the crowd dispersing."

how much one spends. The better professions, responsible executive jobs, even working for a well-known company like General Motors, and a few skilled manual jobs tend to yield status in terms of the job itself. But, as Roethlisberger and Dickson point out, industrial jobs are becoming so specialized that many carry no identifiable status outside the plant: "Modern industry," they say, "has created literally thousands of . . . new occupations, for which there exist no occupational names that have any social significance outside of the particular industry, factory, or even department, in many cases. As a consequence, the wages attaching to these jobs become the most important outer symbol of their social value to the community." [4] And, one may add: the most important outer symbol of the worker's social status in the community. The results flowing from such a situation of job anonymity, as Rexford G. Tugwell has remarked, are pervasive throughout our society. "Our social groups are consuming groups, this is the difficulty. We have almost completely divorced our producing lives from our social lives. At home and among our friends we have no social approval for our productive efforts, and so our neighbors and, tragically, our very wives and children come to estimate us according to our incomes, and not only according to our incomes, but according to the evidence we show of power to spend. Income is inferred from expenditures. So it happens that our social approvals depend upon the limousines of life." [5]

What this adds up to is that, lacking a positive philosophy of groups and of significance, the necessary social sorting out in our culture is allowed to become a dependent function of the central insecurity of our culture, our economic insecurity. Presumably, a positive philosophy of social sorting would, among other things, seek to diminish insecurity by building rich, diversified, positive social living around all potentially constructive human interests.

The second half of the norm for social grouping posed above concerned the active mutual relations of the social groups within a society to the purposes of the society. It was suggested that the social sorting

[4] *Management and the Worker,* Harvard University Press, 1939, p. 574.

[5] "The Distortion of Economic Incentives," *International Journal of Ethics,* April, 1924.

be such as to encourage the groups that are formed to find their places within a positive structure of common social goals. Here one runs at once on the difficulty that our culture has no philosophy of common social goals. Private capitalism in the economic sphere and *laissez faire* in government envisage only a loose structure of live-and-let-live in the pursuit of personal gain. Under this straggling system, in a general weather of insecurity, the grand affirmations of democracy—freedom, equality, and brotherhood—have lost their original positive quality and are today more commonly lived negatively. Freedom becomes freedom of one's person and property from infringement by others. Equality, loosely imputed to everybody, becomes the legal justification for exploitation among persons who are factually unequal in ability and power. Brotherhood becomes a network of offensive and defensive pressure groups. It is a commentary on the extent to which American life has lost touch with the grand purposes of democracy that the chief demand for the postwar domestic world that we read about today in the advertisements in our press is for the return to *individual* enterprise, *i.e.*, the right to go it alone as an economic man.

Although thoughtful men know the bankruptcy of trying to sort out society and to hang a society together around the private scramble for gain, the master social formula of our society continues to be: "Each for himself, and God for all of us, as the elephant said as he danced among the chickens." And "planning" in the United States, *i.e.*, social-goal defining, is today almost entirely economic. This is based on the theory that the only goals for society worth worrying about are economic, and that society will "happen" in the best of all possible ways if we only take care of its economic base.

Lacking clearly stated and positive common *social* goals, and depending chiefly on private and therefore competitive goals in the central economic sphere, we have but meagre basis for orienting one group to another. As a result, groups in American life tend to grind competitively against each other as harsh and unimaginative extensions of the individual competition on which the society is founded. Groups do what individuals do: they largely orient themselves on the axis of power in economic prowess; that is, a faulty theory of the individual in society writes itself large in a system of offensive and defensive groups, and these groups pile themselves up into classes.

So, to sum up group-forming in our American culture: we have no positive theory of group sorting; the resulting sorting we do have is too casual and partial in most cases to support the individual's need for diversified and rounded growth; it tends to emphasize humanly false and trivial likenesses along the money scale of values at the expense of more significant likenesses; from the standpoint of society's needs, it fails to encourage a richly articulated and positive social system; and, by emphasizing humanly nonsignificant lines of association, it develops a class structure based on coercive power—a structure that denies the possibility of building a creative society with significant common purposes.

Even in the economic sphere, around which our joining is so heaped up, this kind of social system is not working. The central theme of *Management and Morale*[6] by Dr. Roethlisberger of the Harvard Business School is that there has been a progressive deterioration in the capacity of men to work together. I shall not stop to dwell here on the free-wheeling aggression this sort of situation turns loose to express itself in our social life in all sorts of ways like anti-Semitism.

2. The norm I suggested at the outset for status giving in democratic society involved a status hierarchy open throughout to all, depending solely on capacity and willingness to contribute to the society's objectives, and with no tolerance of the right of any group to confer special status on itself and to restrict access from below.

In *The Theory of Business Enterprise* Veblen describes how Western society has made the transition from group work to contiguous money-making, while still retaining the original justification of the individual's effort as contributing to the common welfare.[7] I have already mentioned the absence of significant common social goals in our culture. This absence of collective focus would be too scandalous to be tolerated if squarely faced. So, as Veblen notes,

[6] Harvard University Press, 1941.

[7] *Op. cit.* (New York, 1904), pp. 290–291.

we still pretend that there is a 1:1 correlation between acquiring private property and social contribution. In this sense, Mr. Eric Johnston can claim that in the United States the entire hierarchy of status is open to all on the basis of capacity and willingness to contribute to society's objectives.

Need I say that private money-making is not necessarily a contribution to social welfare; that money-making is a wizened personal and social objective; and that in our culture, with its clotted property power, the entire hierarchy of status is not open to all on the basis of capacity and willingness to contribute to democratic society? Even in the United States, education is not freely open to capacity. See in this connection any distribution of intelligence by occupation. As the open frontier economy of the nineteenth century has receded, class factors have come more and more to define one's social fate. Consider this statement in the Senate Temporary National Economic Committee's monograph No. 11 on "Bureaucracy and Trusteeship in Large Corporations": ". . . It is widely recognized that substantial opportunity for promotion does not exist for a large proportion of the workers in either large or small concerns. . . . Most of them, therefore, must look forward to remaining more or less at their current levels despite the havoc this may visit upon the American tradition of 'getting ahead.' "[8]

There are only two ways of achieving status in human society: by ascription and by achievement.[9] The first, status by birth, is irrelevant and inimical to democracy; but we have it, based on the institution of private property. The second type of status is both narrowed and dominated, with equally bad results for democracy, by our constriction of achievement so largely to the aggressive acquisition of property.

A humanly rich and democratic society would diversify achievement so as to encourage it in every line of human endeavor expressing and contributing to socially significant human living. Equal status would be awarded across the whole varied front of significant contributions to society. That we manifestly do not do.

[8] P. 55.

[9] See Ralph Linton, *The Study of Man*, Appleton-Century, 1936, p. 115.

One may object to what I have been saying on the ground that I omit mention of exceptions to these rather dour conclusions. I do so because there is urgent need today to make summary over-all appraisals that get beyond the hopeful fondling of exceptions to deep general tendencies. Or one may protest that it all depends on how one looks at things; that from one angle things may look one way, but from another they look different. If this latter argument is an appeal for social relativism, I am completely opposed to such tolerant relativism in regard to matters crucial to the life of democracy. Individualism has encouraged social relativism as a vast and blowsy suspension of judgment about society so long as business is good. But in this year of fat war profits and the "Little Steel" formula, of Russian advance and British-American fumbling in Italy, of black markets and chiseling on gasoline, of economic pressure groups jockeying in Washington to rig things in their favor after the war, of Aurelio returned to the bench by New York City democracy, of the sharply mounting Negro problem and anti-Semitism—in such a year, I see no room for tolerant relativism.

I was in England this past summer. My experience in Manchester epitomized the confusions which an Institute for Religious Studies such as yours faces in attacking such problems in such a culture as I have been describing. That city is, as you know, the historic home of nineteenth-century liberalism. And yet, so far has Manchester moved in realism regarding the modern scene that some prominent businessmen asked me about Mr. Eric Johnston, who had recently visited the city, "In what era does your Mr. Eric Johnston think he is living, with his belief in the return to economic liberalism?" And yet in this same city people told me I ought to learn about "the new Manchester movement." I did. It is a movement backed by leading manufacturers and businessmen of Manchester and aiming to spread to similar groups over England. Its purpose is to meet the needs of the time by "a return to the fundamental principles of Christianity." [10] That, I submit, is just problem-dodging. No great and fundamental change in "the sickness of an acquisitive society" can be made pri-

[10] See *The Need of the Day,* Sherratt and Hughes, 34 Cross Street, Manchester. 1943. 6d.

marily or centrally by pressing the claims of religion. We have tried that line for a very long time—since long before John Stuart Mill wrote: "I confess I am not charmed with the ideal of life held out by those who think that the normal state of human beings is that of struggling to get on; that the trampling, crushing, elbowing, and treading on each other's heels which form the existing type of social life, are the most desirable lot of human kind. . . ." Despite nearly a century of trying since his day to curb and soften the system by which we live, were Mill alive in our era of growing monopoly, ruthlessness, and cartel collusion and of recurrent world-wide economic wars, I suspect that, rather than seeing improvement in the charmless system by which we live, he would be appalled by our progress-in-reverse.

Religious people can help to change the group problems of our culture and our undemocratic status system, but not primarily by appeals to "brotherhood" or "religious morality," and certainly not by dismissing professors from religious colleges for calling Franco a Fascist.[11] If we are interested in a democratic society composed of

[11] This refers to the dismissal of Dr. Francis E. McMahon by the University of Notre Dame, announced in the press the day this paper was delivered as an address before the Institute for Religious Studies, November 9, 1943.

Ed. In view of the controversy over the McMahon case we think it proper to give the reader the respective statements of the two main parties to it.

On November 9, 1943, Dr. McMahon issued a statement in which he said:

"There is no question of Catholic faith or morals involved, nor do I question the personal integrity or patriotism of the authorities. I do question their judgment about the meaning of free speech and academic freedom, and their interpretation of the effect my work has upon the good name of the university. Likewise I question their appreciation of political factors in world affairs. . . .

"The specific accusations are somewhat vague. It was pointed out to me, however, that I had called Franco a fascist and that I had declared that communism in recent years had been a minor menace compared to nazism. They indicated that they did not want the name of the university associated with the promulgation of these views.

"There is no personal animosity involved, simply a difference in the meaning of free speech."

On that same date, Father Hugh O'Donnell, President of the University, also issued a statement to the press in which he said:

"A rising volume of protests have for some months indicated to the administration that wittingly or unwittingly, Dr. McMahon's individual pronouncements in matters which many Americans consider controversial were being fortified by his identification with the university and in many instances were being interpreted as the university's stand.

(*Continued on next page*)

co-operating groups giving constructive expression to all men's varied significant interests and assigning status on the basis of constructive social contribution, you and I as people who believe in religion must throw our energies into the active fight to displace our present institutional system by a genuinely democratic one. The unfinished business of democracy involves centrally the extension of the democratic process to our economy. And unless religious institutions and their members are prepared to enter this fight to build more democracy by dissolving the clotted power of private property, we people who meet together like this to talk about the applicability of religious values to the ills of society and to resolve things like anti-Semitism by building mutual understanding are largely just whistling in the wind. We live in the midst of a gigantic power struggle, a struggle as to whether societies will move toward more all-out big-business dominance or toward more all-out democracy. It is this struggle that will determine the character of our social system and the future of the things we value. And it is in this struggle that men who seek to remedy society's angry unsocial behavior belong.

BIBLIOGRAPHY

Lynd, Robert S., *Knowledge for What?* Chapters 3, 5, 6.

Lynd, Robert S., "The Implications of Economic Planning for Sociology," *Sociological Review,* February, 1944.

Tawney, R. H., *Equality.*

"It is our policy that only the president of Notre Dame may appropriately express the university's position on such matters when an expression is considered advisable. We consider Dr. McMahon a competent professor of Philosophy and like all other faculty members certainly entitled to his individual opinion and expression. But in our effort to separate the university's identity on these questions from his own it was at last necessary to ask for his resignation.

"Dr. McMahon was simply requested to submit a list of his speaking engagements, an account of his press releases, and the contents of his addresses so that precautions might be suggested by the university administration for separating the name and influence of Notre Dame from Dr. McMahon's position. This single purpose of the procedure was made thoroughly clear to Dr. McMahon.

"Differences of opinion as to his interpretation of Franco, fascism and communism are really incidental to the primary issue which resolved itself into Notre Dame's unwillingness to continue to sponsor by implication, at least, such individual views of a member of the faculty."

VIII

GROUPS AND ECONOMIC ADVANTAGE

BY

JAMES P. GIFFORD, LL.B.

Assistant Professor of Law and Assistant to the Dean of the Law School, Columbia University

Normally such a topic as Groups and Economic Advantage calls for a paper bristling with statistics designed to prove scientifically what everybody knows—that within any community there are racial, religious, and economic groups which, on the whole, are either better or worse off than other groups. The rich are few and the poor are many. The fact that every superior person in recorded history has been concerned with the problem of poverty proves only this—that, either no workable device has yet been invented to correct this evil, or, if invented, such device has not been put into effect largely because the rich want to remain rich and a great many of the poor want the chance to get rich if possible. But we are living in a time when some of the rich and most of the poor are no longer acquiescing in the inevitableness of this division but have experimented and are attempting to work out social devices to bring about a greater measure of economic equality. That the idea of the Four Freedoms has not been laughed to scorn shows that men in general are inspired by a hope, which, to some, seems to verge almost on madness, that somehow, in some way, all over the world, all men can reap the benefits of an abundance which the earth seems willing to afford if only man can use sufficient intelligence and energy to secure and to distribute its products wisely and humanely.

But, knowing the human capacity for selfishness, greed, and inertia, it is well to consider this entire problem of economic differences among groups along very broad lines. For if we confine ourselves to a single community or to a single nation we cannot, today, remain unaware of the fact that no one nation can attain great economic prosperity without arousing among other nations the same evils which exist within a single nation when one section of its citizens is fabulously rich and the rest are appallingly poor. For the insecurity, envy, and fear which lead to class wars within a nation are part of the powerful impulses toward the kind of international conflict the world is now enduring. Although it is probable that violent conflicts between societies or between groups within a single society cannot be completely eliminated, because there comes a time when any group will fight either for some advantage or against some disadvantage, it would be the part of reason to try to organize our world so as to postpone as long as possible the more obvious causes which compel a resort to arms. That, I take it, is the underlying thought behind all schemes of international co-operation which blossom in every bookstore almost weekly. All such schemes represent the hope that men can act rationally even though such hope represents an emotional triumph over past experience. One source of some expectation of rational behavior lies in the growing realization that, if mankind does not act rationally, there is a very fair chance it will succeed in completely destroying itself. As soon as every person in every nation begins to understand that it is possible that he can be bombed out of existence from any other point on this planet, then people may decide to act as if all men were brothers. It is not a wholly pleasant thought that the pilot, the bombardier, and the airplane designer may be more potent factors than the somewhat divided doctrines of religious teachers in producing a sense of unity among mankind. But the ways of the Lord and of the devil have never been easy to divine.

In discussing the topic before us, although one might debate whether it is an advantage to be born very rich, scarcely anyone will deny that it is a serious disadvantage to be born very poor. It is grimly interesting and informative to compare within a single city the statistics of rich and poor districts as to infant mortality, death rates from tuberculosis, and contagious diseases, and to conclude that a fortunate selection of one's parents is undoubtedly the best assurance of a reasonably endurable existence. There are, of course, circles within circles, and strata even among the poor. In the South, for example, it is probable that many of the so-called poor white trash are as badly off as the poorest among the Negroes, but the whites have the consolation of belonging to the socially and economically dominant group, which comfort cannot be measured in economic terms. In fact, many of the advantages or disadvantages of belonging to a particular group are by no means purely economic. Novels of the late nineteenth and early part of the twentieth century frequently dealt with the theme of the *nouveau riche* trying to buy his or his wife's way into an imaginary heaven of social success. Nor is it a theme that will ever die, for there will always be the self-recognized ins and the envious outs. Even today in the Soviet Republic a tuition fee is imposed for high-school training, and, although this arises as a war measure to divert more youngsters toward specialized technical training, it may produce sharp and lasting group divisions in the future.

But granted that in any society there will always be prestige groups envied by all others, our American society up to the outbreak of World War II was definitely tending toward establishing prestige very largely on the basis of income. A college education was a good thing because it assured one a higher income. College presidents collected figures to show that holders of Phi Beta Kappa keys were certain to do better in professional schools than their ostensibly less gifted brethren. In professional schools, particularly in law schools, students struggled for top honors because honor students were practically guaranteed positions in the big law firms of large cities whose partners had incomes in terms of five and frequently six figures. This tendency has by no means disappeared. The newspapers recently published figures showing that the doctors were, on the whole, making more money than the lawyers, a complaint which had been heard from the lawyers in one community as early as 1937. The successful minister was he who was called to a large city church and could command a sizable staff of highly paid parish workers.

The receipt of a large income is, in itself, no evil thing. It is no crime to grow prosperous and, in a society such as ours was tending to become, it was almost impossible for an energetic and intelligent man to resist the pressure exerted by the social forces with which he was surrounded at every step in his development. Every one of us beyond the age of forty-five can point to numerous boyhood friends who suppressed marked talents, altruistic ideals, or warm, humanizing tendencies to devote a life to becoming a cog in an industrial or financial machine. And if anyone were so priggish or so bold as to comment on the personal or social waste involved, he was definitely regarded as queer because he was thereby criticizing the very structure of society, which exerts a force almost no individual is strong enough to overcome. And the most deplorable feature of the whole picture lies in the fact that those who either by choice or accident swam against the current and engaged in occupations which were sure to allow them to live and die in poverty went about the tasks they loved with a sense of apology, frequently masked by humorous references to their being nothing but an artist, or a teacher, or a musician, as if being such were a disgrace. That in itself is a shameful commentary on a society—that it should produce such warped emotions.

But each society is bound to contain its misfits. It is probable that in every social group there is a residue of incorrigibles, a small percentage who simply will not conform—tough, unresilient individualists—the despair of reformers, pedagogues, idealists, and efficiency experts. In Russia, for example, in a generation which has for twenty-five years grown up under Soviet influences, we find just about the same percentage of voluntary absenteeism as we do in the United States. There is a certain healthy note in all this. It was Emerson who liked the sayers of "No." But on the whole, war teaches us anew a lesson that is both hopeful and terrifying—namely, that by making the correct appeals, a society can be marshalled into extraordinary activity to preserve itself or to achieve supposedly attainable goals. We talk much of the difference in docility between our enemies and ourselves. This seems very debatable ground. There is nothing to show that American soldiers of Japanese, German, or Italian descent have exhibited any less willingness to fight for the United States than Americans of any other racial origin. We can go thus far with Watson and state almost categorically that, if a dozen German children and a dozen English children had, at birth, been transplanted to England and to Germany, they would now be fighting each other, each in the uniform of his foster country. This is not to say that the values held by the contestants are identical. But the illustration forcefully emphasizes the malleability of the human animal and gives hope to those who desire to change society and, perchance, to improve it. Yet, there is something distasteful to an introspectively honest person in attempting to reform someone else. We all realize how much we are the products of a chance heredity and an environment over which we have little control. There is a place in human behavior for self-control and self-development, but they, in themselves, are perhaps more illusory than real. *Capricornia,* that vigorous novel by Xavier Herbert, shows how chance alone can transform the life of a half-caste boy into something fairly tolerable, while his contemporaries, male and female, subjected to the most "pious" of influences, remain rebellious, illiterate savages, endlessly seeking the means to escape into the bush and the relative freedom of its hardships.

But to change society instead of attempting to reform the individual is to change the social environment and to ensure in time that the great mass of individuals will respond to that change. If the internal economics of a group can be arranged so that individual survival does not depend on fierce competitive struggle, then the individuals will change. Values once regarded as important become unimportant and new values take their place. What was once regarded as good now becomes evil and traits formerly regarded as signs of weakness now become qualities worthy of praise. But the difficulty in outlining any program for social change lies in the fact that we cannot find agreement as to the ultimate or final values to be sought. We decried in December, 1941, the softness of the young men and women who, since that time, have seemed quite capable of doing all the hard things necessary to compete with tough Fascists, well-trained Nazis, and tenacious Japanese. Who is sufficiently wise to say whether our young men and women have changed basically or whether this toughness is merely a role they have assumed out of necessity and that, once the war is over, they will go on being what they started out to be before the war overtook them? We know in our hearts that those who return will not be the same, but we do not know in exactly what respects they will be different, for we have found that we did not know the real nature of those in whom some seemed to have so little confidence. Are these young men and women the ones who are really going to change our society? They will form the largest unit that has shared a common emotional experience, that has directed its efforts toward a common danger, and has known the same sense of risking all for a single objective. What kind of society is it probable they will insist on?

Will they, like the mythical soldier in the advertisements, want everything to be the same? That seems somewhat doubtful. Nevertheless, millions of them will have lived in an environment where every physical and many recreational and emotional needs are supplied as a matter of course. For them life insurance is a matter of routine; disability is compensated for; the gap between army and civilian life is going to be bridged (the equivalent of unemployment insurance in civilian life); hospitalization is not only available, it is usually compulsory; diet is carefully planned and the quantity and quality of the food are generally good; allotments are given to families left in difficult circumstances; and organizations exist to help out in emergencies. To our soldiers, the return to a civilian existence which lacks some of these communal methods of protection against the contingencies of existence may seem quite uncivilized and barbaric. And the demand for these safeguards cannot be reasoned away by saying that in war it is necessary to provide these things because the individual is incapable of providing them himself. The truth is that in civilian existence the vast majority of individuals are incapable of providing these essentials. They can only be secured by social action. Suppose there were no such thing as a police force; would the small private guards of the wealthy few be adequate to protect even the wealthy? No one thinks of abolishing the police force or the fire department or the public waterworks or the public parks, museums, or libraries. No one would advocate abolition of the school system. Yet all these essentials are furnished by taking some portion of the income of each person in the community and giving back to the entire community social benefits which would never exist in adequate form if the matter were left to individual initiative.

There is much talk current of preserving the American system of free individual enterprise. That vague phrase, largely used at present as a political stereotype to win as many adherents as possible, deserves some analysis. Free enterprise covers a wide variety of activities. It includes the homesteader who, by endurance and luck, gets a quarter section of land and holds on to it until some railroad or trucking company comes near enough for him to ship his produce to a market at a profit. That group will exist again, if not in this country, certainly in Canada, where plans are already being formed to make farms available to returning soldiers. Free enterprise also includes the huge corporation with established sales outlets all over the country, possessing every patent remotely related to its products, having factories in every center strategically favorable as to transportation, raw materials, and labor, and controlling sufficient funds to maintain expensive research workers in superbly equipped laboratories. Between these extremes lie all the myriad forms of activity —financial, commercial, industrial, professional, and manual—by which men have gained a living in the past and hope to do so again. If all these forms of activity are included under the phrase "free enterprise," then the phrase has little significance. If only some of them are included, then it would make for clearer thinking if we stated exactly which forms of activity are to be kept "free" and, furthermore, just what they are to be kept free from. However, let us leave this interesting task of definition to the contestants in the coming political campaign.

Just now, perhaps, by implication we emphasized too much the effects of army and navy life on the men and women in service. If, for them, that period is nothing but an emotional and intellectual interlude between leaving and resuming an existence regarded as normal, if the period is too short to set up new habits of behavior strong enough to resist the influences which are bound to push them toward a return to peacetime ways of living, then we must look to tendencies which were in existence before the war and were affecting the civilian population at that time.

Let us look, therefore, at certain general social trends which were beginning to take fairly definite shape before World War II and see whether it is probable they will continue after the war. We can best describe those trends by briefly reviewing their history. Today the word feudal is synonymous with everything that is blindly antisocial and reactionary. Yet feudalism had its points. In spite of the absence of modern plumbing and running water, feudalism had a fair degree of social stability. The obligations between lord and villein were mutual. The villein had his rights as well as his duties and in his old age and time of infirmity could not be cruelly cast aside as the employer of the industrial era can even now cast aside an aging employee. As feudalism began to dissolve, the transition in human relations from status to contract, in the interlude between the break-up of feudalism and the coming of the Industrial Revolution, brought with it an increasing sense of individual freedom which coincided with the greatest period of exploration and expansion the world has known. But the coming of the Industrial Revolution saw the beginning of the modern social tendency, in every country it touched, to concentrate wealth in a few hands and to leave a large portion of the population without anything to offer but its labor. In England the then existing division between owners and workers was sharply accentuated. The Revolution in France was aimed at destroying the legal inequalities between aristocrat and peasant. Once these were removed it was believed that economic equality would take care of itself. But France began to follow the inevitable pattern in spite of the fact that a very large portion of its population remained in the class of peasant landowners. In the United States, the tendency toward sharp divisions between classes was greatly retarded by the long period of expansion which had not wholly ceased as late as 1914. After 1918, however, the divisions began to be accentuated and by 1933, after four years of economically depressed conditions, it was evident to many, except a few political leaders, that there was a sizable portion of the population which would need immediate protection against unemployment.

The relatively complete indifference of employers toward the social welfare of employees which marked the beginnings and the early decades of the Industrial Revolution began to be offset by measures of a socialistic nature. On the whole, Europe was far ahead of the United States in enacting laws to provide unemployment insurance, workmen's compensation, sickness insurance, maternity benefits, and the like. Although the United States had given its citizens the political power to create these methods of social protection, the necessity seemed absent, the urge to compel their widespread enactment had not arisen in full force until after 1929. The legislation of the past decade, however, was largely a process of catching up with Europe. There are those who still mourn the existence of the laws which seem to them utterly at variance with their picture of that lovely vague thing, the American way of life. One feels sad for these romantic persons who still believe that by industry, ability, and brains the son of any workman can rise to the highest financial or political level. But such persons fail to distinguish between the possible (and it is still possible) and the probable. A healthy, dynamic society cannot live without a dream, but a society to be strong must also distinguish between a dream and a delusion. And the reality is that the great bulk of our population will not advance very far economically, although the total income of the country may increase tremendously.

What is the remedy in order to produce a society where the individual, no matter how humble his economic or social origin, can count on a certain minimum measure of protection against the contingencies of life such as disease and unemployment, which may otherwise blot him out like an unwanted animal? The remedy is, of course, a redistribution of wealth, a term widely used, rarely defined, and usually misunderstood or misapplied. The redistribution of wealth is a process that has gone on ever since the first generous person gave alms to the first unfortunate. The church insisted on a redistribution of wealth in so far as tithes were used to help the poor. But redistribution did not assume its modern and most powerful form until the introduction of the progressive income tax. Although every individual who pays rent or buys goods subject to tax is contributing to governmental revenue, the progressive income tax has made it evident to all that every member of society may be compelled to contribute to public funds in proportion to the income he makes or receives. This is not the occasion to discuss or justify the theory of progressive taxation. It has come to stay in some form or other, just as the recent pronouncements of Mr. Willkie show that the various forms of social protection introduced both by and prior to the Roosevelt administration will remain a part of the political and economic program of both major parties from now on.

These changes are not fortuitous. They were and are a necessary answer to the demand for security which the economically disfranchised portion of the United States and of every other modern industrialized nation had been making from at least the beginning of the twentieth century. Not all countries made the same answer. Russia tried to meet the situation through the ideas of Communism or, more realistically, State Capitalism. Germany met the problem largely through an imitation of Italy's Fascism and Russia's State Capitalism, with its characteristic addition of military conquest. Italy adopted its own forms of social control coupled with vicious attacks against opposition. England first, and later the United States, introduced collective bargaining and various forms of social insurance to buttress the individual against the disasters which individually he was powerless to overcome.

The purpose of these methods of redistribution were all similar—they were all assertions of the basic proposition, "Follow these methods and you will achieve as much happiness as mortals are capable of enjoying." That, of course, is an expression of faith. But the skeptical eye of modern man constantly insists on looking beyond faith to works. Are these schemes for equalizing the economic positions of social groups anything more than the bread and circuses of the Roman emperors, an attempt to satisfy the normal desire of every animal to meet its needs with as little effort as possible? Will such measures produce a nation of partial parasites who, deprived of any need for individual initiative or inventiveness, will fall prey to the members of hardier nations capable of adapting themselves to changing conditions? These are hard questions, questions which every parent has asked himself in reference to the upbringing of his children, and which every teacher has asked in connection with the instruction of his pupils. The continued existence of any group depends upon the ability of the individuals in that group to meet the changing economic, climatic, social, and ideologic conditions, all of which move like a continuous wave ready to engulf those incapable of meeting its onslaught or of diverting its energies to their own ends. James Watt, as he evolved the steam engine, could not have known that he was assuring the economic dominance of those nations which learned to use it. But as Max Lerner has well said, history is written by the survivors. If the Moslems had conquered Europe, the history of Europe would have been written by them. So our nation, in fact all nations, must today read the signs correctly—must have both the wisdom and good fortune to be able to draw the dividing lines properly between the social necessity of affording the great mass of men the stability and security essential to a strong and wholesome existence and the equally important social necessity of maintaining sufficient insecurity to stimulate imagination, industry, and a sense of the hard realities of mortal existence so that others will not stamp out and dominate the relatively free societies which still remain the last, best hope of man.

For there is nothing in our pride in ourselves or in our vast industrial organization which can guarantee our survival or even the continuance of our industrial system. Perhaps it is futile to look too far ahead—but there are recent warnings that the end of our present supply of oil is but a short way off in terms of historical time. We blithely assume we shall find or invent a substitute. But what if we do not? Then, our machine age will grind to a standstill in a few short hours and we can envision the aborigines of Northern Australia or the primitive peasants of China suddenly becoming the meek who shall inherit the earth. No Jeremiah will ever be popular, but as we approach a period when great choices are to be made, we must remind ourselves that in our humble place as animals whose function seems to be to adapt ourselves to the natural conditions of this planet, we must first and last remain meek rather than arrogant toward such conditions as cannot be changed, but at the same time we must remain invincibly determined to attempt to control what can be controlled in order that existence may be as tolerable as possible for an ever-increasing majority on this potentially bountiful earth.

IX

GROUP DISCRIMINATION IN INDUSTRY

BY

MARK STARR

Educational Director, International Ladies' Garment Workers Union

There are at least two reasons why a consideration of group discrimination in industry is both timely and important. In the first place, you will recall that Hitler in *Mein Kampf* boasted that conquering the United States would be "an inside job" because he counted on the internal disunity among the many races and nationalities which, in his opinion, had not yet learned to work together.

We have, as you know, in the United States about 13,000,000 Negroes, 3,500,000 Mexicans, 361,000 American Indians, 127,000 Japanese, 77,000 Chinese, and 45,000 Filipinos. In Hawaii there are 319,000 people of color. These "brothers under the skin" are in addition to the millions of white immigrants into the U.S.A. No wonder Goebbels told Rauschning ". . . Nothing will be easier than to produce a bloody revolution in America. No other country has so many social and racial tensions. We shall be able to play on many strings there. North America is a medley of races."

So far, at least, we have disappointed Hitler's hopes of racial conflict. Let us work the harder to make this prophecy of his work in reverse. However, we shall do this only if we grasp the nettle boldly and not attempt to overlook how discrimination has weakened the all-out productive effort necessary to overcome the Nazi-Fascist powers.

The other great reason for the urgency of tackling the problem of discrimination against minorities is the fact that the United States, as a member of the United Nations, must now give leadership in reorganizing the world into new political units. It does not matter whether you think in terms of a regional plan; whether you support the Culbertson Plan of world federal government with its division of the world into eleven areas with a superstate president and congress and an international army based on the quota principle; or whether you merely think in terms of the United Nations with its big four—United States, Britain, Soviet Russia, and China—dominating the world situation. In every case there is a greater need than ever to understand the problems of our brothers under the skin in the Far East, where more than half of the world's population lives. We cannot unscramble the omelet and nothing can ever put the millions of China and the millions of India back into their prewar position. The recent great historic conferences of Stalin, Chiang, Churchill, and Roosevelt only set the stage of operations.

Some of us hope that in the United States not only shall we be able to pioneer and secure social planning plus the Bill of Rights in our internal life, but that the great unprecedented opportunity which the United States affords and demonstrates, for a successful commingling of races and nations on the basis of mutual understanding, will be seized to the immeasurable benefit of humanity.

These are the days that try men's minds as well as their souls and there is no place for the sunshine soldier and the summer patriot who cannot rise above the accidents of their birth and see the modern world as created by the age of aviation and the annihilation of distance and barriers which hitherto kept mankind isolated inside tribal frontiers. That world view has to operate in every workshop as well as in conferences and parliaments.

The war has brought many of our concealed problems out into the light of day. I think we should welcome this. No improvements have ever been made without conflicts and struggle. Even the defeats so far administered by our reactionary Congress to the attempts to destroy the poll tax have resulted in a greater publicity, and some of the Southern states have been thereby stimulated to take action themselves. When the Northern Negro goes to the South and bucks the peculiar prejudices of the people, there is often bitter friction which has, in some instances, actually caused a loss of life. In the over-all picture, however, the great demand for labor power has enabled the Negro to find his way into many previously lily-white concerns. The Southern Negro, coming to the North, shares in the educational experience of being treated as an equal for the first time.

But the problem should not be confined to minorities which can be distinguished by their color. Of course, color is easy to recognize and there is a greater difficulty of absorption. This, despite the fact that there are cases of "passing over" carried through by light-skinned Negroes and Mexicans.

Carey McWilliams in his book, *Brothers under the Skin,* has well reminded us that we can, if we wish, avoid the race riots which followed World War I. Our problem, he explains, is now more complicated because Japanese, Chinese, and Mexicans are involved. At Pearl Harbor it was members of the yellow race who made the attack. In California there are 500,000 Mexicans and these have their own delinquency problems among the young boys and girls who neither belong to Mexico nor to the United States and who also, incidentally, suffer from the fact that their parents are working and unable to give them the proper parental care and affection. Even before Pearl Harbor, Carey McWilliams points out, there was considerable racial tension on the West Coast, arising from the economic stresses and strains of war time. The Chinese, for example, losing their jobs and their shops through the disturbance in world trade, moved out of Chinatown and went into wartime industries.

The participation of Chiang Kai-shek in the Four-Power Conference indicates a deserved, if somewhat delayed, recognition that China has made a tremendous contribution to saving the ideals of democracy at untold cost to herself. We have become conscious of the Orient; Pearl Buck and the East and West Association endeavor to bring the United States and China more closely together. (The only possible criticism of East and West is that it should be North and South as well, because surely we need to know what is happening in South America and in Canada as well as what is happening in China and India.)

Carey McWilliams reported last spring a growing awareness of the evil of discrimination and intensified protests against it. Although the Federal Government has not exercised to the full its wartime powers, it has made some steps in the right direction to override local prejudice in the name of all-out production.

John Collier, as head of the Bureau of Indian Affairs, Department of the Interior, advocates an Institute of Ethnic Affairs. His policy has been to secure equal access to education, to health, and to every social amenity for all minorities and definitely to provide for this equal access by government action wherever necessary. That surely should be applied to Jewish, Italian, Irish, Catholic, Puerto Rican, West Indian, Mexican, Negro, minorities, and every other group in the United States handicapped by its race, religion, or color.

Carey McWilliams and other experts favor the adoption of a Fair Racial Practices Act, something like the state laws which have already been adopted in New York. *PM* (April 27, 1943) summarized Mr. McWilliam's proposals thus:

> A fair Racial Practices Law, national in scope, defining types of organizations that discriminate and areas of discrimination.
>
> Enabling legislation to enforce the 14th, 15th, and 16th Amendments to the Constitution.
>
> Enforcement of Congressional power to reduce the representation in the Congress of States which discriminate against minorities. They should be made to do this by a national movement.
>
> Creation of an Institute of Ethnic Affairs within the Interior Department to educate the American people by officially spotlighting discriminations.
>
> Co-ordination and study of ways of enforcing the democratic rights of minorities; co-operation with similar groups outside the Government.
>
> Grants to Southern States for public health, housing, libraries, and recreational facilities for minority groups. If the States refuse these aids, the Federal Government should set them up.

There are objections to making men and women behave properly by the compulsion of the law. The American Federation of Labor pleads in its defense, when eloquently and repeatedly criticized by Mr. Randolph of the Pullman Porters, that it cannot exercise coercion against constituent unions which openly or secretly discriminate against Negroes and other races. Certainly it would be good if attitudes could be changed by self-correction just as it would be well if laws were unnecessary owing to perfect education and self-discipline exercised by citizens. However, some element of coercion seems indispensable in any organized community to protect that community from antisocial and dangerous behavior.

Some of the groups which, for example, have been working for the betterment of the Negroes' status by slow educational methods are now beginning to doubt whether they should rely upon that method alone. They note that labor-hating and union-baiting employers now look upon unions in a different way since the Wagner Act made collective bargaining a recognized part of our Constitution.

There would be considerable difficulty of passing the act in the first place, but that itself would be an educational project of the first order. Every argument and every speech in Congress and in the public hearings attendant upon the adoption of such a Fair Racial Practices Act would help to direct public attention upon these acts of treachery against the democratic spirit, and spotlight the danger zones in racial relationships.

Congress, in the opinion of many authorities, has the constitutional right to enforce the Bill of Rights and the Fourteenth Amendment and restore the original interpretation of that Fourteenth Amendment before judge-made law whittled it away. In every instance, where the individual state was obdurate, the Federal Government could step in and provide equal facilities for education, housing, health, etc., under the wartime power which it possesses. Such a law would have much greater power than the Fair Employment Practices Committee, which never had a clear legal basis and was created merely by an executive order of the President.

But wisdom suggests that much can be done by individual action if we know the extent and cause of group discrimination, particularly in its basic manifestation in industry.

The difficulties recently met by the FEPC show both how difficult the road is and how much progress has been made. You will recall that Controller General Warren tried to interpret the word "shall" in the FEPC order as being permissive and not mandatory. Let us hope that he is not called upon to interpret the Ten Commandments: for example, "Thou *shalt* not kill;" "Thou *shalt* not commit adultery;" "Thou *shalt* not steal." Presumably he would maintain that obedience to these commands is also optional. And please note that in the New Testament it does not say "Thou shalt love thy *white* neighbor as thyself."

Why shelter behind weasel words and not acknowledge that our administrators were welshing on the promise of long-delayed justice to our fellow Americans whose skin is darker in its pigment? If such evasions are to be attempted, let us abandon any pretence and invite Hitler in to apply directly his racial nonsense about the superior Nordic and Aryan races. We shape the end of this war by the methods we use to fight it. We cannot do justice to the ideal of the United Nations if we stigmatize men of color and allow Controller General Warren to try to find a let-out for lily-white corporations, seeking to defeat the purpose of the FEPC. While President Roosevelt reversed the decision, Warren is still in office.

I hope that all of you read the story in the *New Republic* of November 8 about an incident reported from Jamaica:

The most talked of incident in Jamaica is that of the Negro labor foreman who, pressed for time, dashed into a lavatory labeled WHITE and was met with the fist of one of the Southerners as he came out. Quick as a boxer throwing a counter punch, he knocked the American to the ground. He went for his coat and was on the way to the pay office when the American called him back. Shake, he said, and forget it. They shook hands. Today they are friends.

Frankly, we should like incidents of that sort in the United States to teach Americans in a forcible fashion the implications of their own Constitution; although, of course, as a person with a vested interest in adult education, I should like to see education making fisticuffs unnecessary and teaching the lesson in a less painful way.

I blush in shame that the leaders of the American Federation of Labor are not more active in educating their constituent unions to cease the crimes which they commit against every ideal of Americanism and human decency, when they discriminate against Negro workers. Let us not, as the fairer-skinned members of humanity, forget that we are at this moment in the minority and that the common people of the world are on the march.

While in Britain in August-September of this year, the question second in order of occurrence put to me in meetings was, "Why do Americans discriminate against Negroes?" Naturally in my reply I referred to color bars in India and Africa before I explained the history behind our unfair treatment of the Negro. I suggested that we should not repent the other fellow's sins but do something about our own. Pedagogues must not be content to regurgitate polysyllabics. Liberals must come out of their storm cellars and their armchairs of academic ease and fight, if necessary, for legal compulsion to save the American principles of equality of opportunity for all men. They must do this just as they must revise their ideas about giving freedom of speech to those who openly advocate its destruction.

What effective propaganda based on facts of racial discrimination can Tokio make! Can you not hear them telling the millions of colored folk in the Far East that Uncle Sam wants black men to kill yellow men for the sake of white men, while the same white men will not give the Negro an equal break? In the Digest of FEPC Hearings on Railroads there are listed copies of transcriptions of radio broadcasts and editorials from Germany, Italy, and Japan based on discrimination against the Negro in the United States.

And we must all do something now to stop any further sneak-thief grab at the powers of the FEPC. Let us say in no uncertain terms to Controller Warren and to Washington: You *shall* be just to American citizens. Let us say to our representatives in Congress and to our President in no uncertain voice that the Committee on Fair Employment Practices must be made a legal, permanent, and more powerful agency to clean from the United States the dark stain of racial discrimination!

FEPC deserves praise for its decision of November 30 to order 22 railroads and seven unions to cease and desist discriminating against Negroes. In *The New York Times* (Dec. 3, 1943) the Brotherhood of Sleeping Car Porters hailed the decision in a full page "ad" which reported encouraging instances of co-operation between black and white railroad workers:

Reading this record, one sees again and again, through the murk of discrimination and fear, a white hand extended in the fellowship of a responsible and dangerous craft, and always a black hand outstretched to clasp it.

But the fight is not over; that arch union-baiter, Representative Howard W. Smith, has started to undermine the decision. In view of the successful maneuvering over the poll tax, Smith may be able to get Congress to support Controller Warren instead of President Roosevelt.

Criticism of President Roosevelt on the Negro issue is not confined to Southern reactionaries. Elliott Janeway, writing in the December 1943 *Fortune* on the President's trials and errors, says:

From the standpoint of the national welfare, perhaps the most tragic—and explosive—illustration of the President's self-imposed isolation is the Negro problem. The terrible Negro crisis brewing in this country today is the result of many causes and bears on many vital problems. Not the least ominous of the phenomena it reflects is the growing Balkanization of the United States into conflicting minorities, none understanding the point of view or granting the good will of the others, each becoming more and more disposed to violence against the others. In the case of the Negroes, what matters primarily is not that the Negro crisis is bad for the President or for any other politician. It is that the Negroes, having lost their original faith in the will and ability of the party of Abraham Lincoln to absorb them into this democracy, have now to all intents and purposes come to feel that they were naïve in transferring their faith to Franklin Roosevelt.

For if any mood is dominant among them today it is that no white man or party can be trusted to give them what they want, and that they will not be satisfied with anything less than full justice, as they see it, immediately—even though the majority of whites are obviously not going to win this even for themselves. Up to this point, one of Mr. Roosevelt's truly great political achievements was to persuade the Negroes that they would advance their own cause by working in alliance with the underprivileged white groups supporting him. Today this faith is gone. In its place, open two-way hostility is flaring up all around the country between the Negroes and organized labor—hostility so bitter and passionate that in many, many cases Mr. Roosevelt will have to choose between alienating labor as the price of mending his fences with the Negroes, and alternatively, letting the anti-Negro unions have their way and admitting that the Negroes are lost to him. No Democrat can win without pyramiding Negro votes on top of white labor votes.

Moreover, Mr. Roosevelt's southern supporters fear that he will give the Negroes so much before the election that their position will become untenable back home. Some of them, sharing the suspicion of the Republicans who feel that Mr. Roosevelt and Mr. Willkie are fundamentally alike, even fear that, if Willkie fails to win the Republican nomination, Mr. Roosevelt will offer him the vice-presidential nomination; this, they feel, would cost Mr. Roosevelt important southern support. But whatever else may be thought in the South, very few Southerners are aware of the extent to which the Negroes have been moving into bitter opposition against the Roosevelt Administration. That representative Negroes could speak of him more bitterly than the most unrepresentative Tory Southerners, that they could be more against him than against men who had never promised them anything or, for example, given them any housing, is a fact that is incomprehensible below the Mason-Dixon Line. But, again, what matters is not so much that Mr. Roosevelt is caught between these conflicting forces as that at a time when the United States should be dedicated to a single purpose, two such politically powerful minorities should be unable to compromise their conflicting claims, and they are acting as if they would be unresponsive to any genuinely national leadership if such were miraculously to appear.

The industrial discrimination against the Negro should not obscure discrimination against women, against Jews, and against Catholics.[1]

Statistics are difficult to obtain about the extent of discrimination in general industry. When the Little Rock, Ark., Chamber of Commerce advertised in 1937, "Ideal labor conditions—open shop—ample American labor always available at Southern wage level," was that discrimination?

Dorothy Norman, columnist in the *New York Post,* says:

[1] (Incidentally it is sad to note that in some cases where Catholics or Protestants officially have power, their leaders put discrimination into reverse and through clerical controls in politics penalize those who do not accept their ideas. In Soviet Russia where racism is outlawed, political opponents are liquidated.)

Of 400 plants investigated by the New York State Committee on Discrimination, only 229 employ Negroes. These 400 plants had 401,375 employees, of which 4,700 were Negroes—just over 1 per cent. Of the plants employing Negroes, 94 employed less than 14, the majority four or fewer. One third of all the plants visited by the committee have four or fewer Negroes in any and all capacities.

An unpublished report presented to the War Manpower Commission in November, 1943, said in part:

> Out of 227 local transportation companies—representing 80 per cent of total employment in that industry—only eight employ Negro operators.
>
> In the textile mills in Spartanburg, S.C., employers are refusing to hire locally available Negroes and at the same time are insisting that the Government provide additional housing facilities to house in-migrant white workers.
>
> In the Buffalo-Niagara Falls area, out of a total of 80 firms representing the important war industries, 45 per cent of the 9,490 Negroes employed in May were in five firms in the blast furnaces, steel works, and rolling machines industry.
>
> In none of the tight labor markets of the North does there appear a significant use of skilled Negro workers in war industry as a whole.
>
> Available data indicate that the employment of Negro women is limited to a small number of firms in a few industries. . . . In the Baltimore area 75.5 per cent of the 2,249 Negro women employed were working in only four establishments.
>
> In acute labor-shortage areas of the South, Negroes are principally used as unskilled labor. In none of (them) has there developed a trend toward upgrading Negroes to new occupations, with the possible exception of one shipyard.
>
> These situations and many others, says the WMC report, "have not been met because the practice has been not to employ Negroes where serious opposition has appeared."

Herbert R. Northrup reveals the dark side of the trade-union record in discrimination when he lists (*Journal of Political Economy,* June, 1943) fifteen unions which specifically exclude Negroes by explicit rules or rituals. Of these only nine are important, and of the nine five belong to the AFL and four are independent. Five other unions, AFL affiliates, "usually deny admittance to Negroes by tacit consent." Nine others permit Negroes to join but limit their rights. As one might expect, remembering Samuel Gompers and noting the religious affiliation of prominent leaders of the AFL and CIO, Mr. Northrup found only one small insignificant union of less than 500 members, the Wire Weavers Association, which admits "white Christian males" only and charges aliens an admission fee of $1000. Mr. Northrup's evidence in the FEPC case against the Southern railroads, his forthcoming book on organized labor and the Negro worker, and the speeches at the AFL conventions are among the best sources of information about what the unions are doing to eliminate discrimination. The ILGWU in the AFL and the Auto Workers, CIO, are outstanding in their attempts to give the Negroes fair treatment and unite them with their fellow workers in a struggle for betterment.

Critics of the unions should always examine whether opposition to Negroes by workers is xenophobic prejudice or based upon the use of the Negro as a scab or to undercut labor standards. For example, Henry Ford's extensive employment of Negro workers was mixed in motivation. The Auto Workers inherited headaches on this point but courageously did the right thing.

The Auto Workers Union estimates that ten per cent of its million members are Negroes. Here is a case where union leaders are doing an educational job. Listen to R. J. Thomas speaking to white workers at the Packard plant who had struck against the upgrading of Negroes:

> Negroes pay a dollar a month dues, the same as any other union member. Negroes have fought for this organization the same as others. Negroes will fight for it in the future. And still some people ask why Negroes should be upgraded.
>
> At a Packard local meeting there were large groups of women workers protesting the upgrading of Negroes. Those women forget that a few months ago women were discriminated against in our industry. We still have to fight in some plants for equal pay for women. If any group should support our fight against discrimination more than anybody else, it is our women workers.
>
> We talk about the North and South differentials in wages and living

standards. The white people of the South thought that Negroes should work for a cheaper wage. Then the poor whites were brought down to the Negroes' level due to that kind of wage competition.

I have given an ultimatum to the Packard workers that they must go back to work. I am going to make that ultimatum stronger and if it means that large numbers of white workers are going to get fired, then that is exactly what's going to happen.

This International union is not going to retreat from that position.

Reuther and other UAW leaders, according to Frank Winn in the Fall issue of the *Antioch Review,* do this because they recognize that:

1. An American labor movement can never be completely or even nearly effective without the active support of that large body of workers.

2. To accept discrimination or segregation divides and weakens the ranks of labor and puts a drag on the advancement of living standards for all workers.

3. To exclude Negroes, as has been and still is done by many unions outside the CIO, automatically creates a tremendous and dangerous strike-breaking, union-busting force.

The officers of the UAW–CIO do not deceive themselves that when a white worker signs an application card he automatically sloughs off the race prejudice which has been most probably instilled in him since he was a child, even though the union's constitution says it will not tolerate discrimination. And they have learned by bitter experience that appeals to that kind of worker on the high plane of brotherhood usually go unheeded.

They have also learned, however, that when they can show the same worker that discrimination is a threat to his living standards and working conditions, he is inclined to subordinate his prejudice and accept the Negro as a fellow worker and fellow union member. Once that hurdle is crossed, the white worker begins to perceive the unreasonableness of his emotional prejudice and the brotherhood idea starts to make sense.

Among many interesting examples of how objections to Negro

upgrading and the introduction of Negro women into Ford's are overcome Frank Winn quotes the following case:

Here is a typical example of how objections from white workers are met and overcome: In an important Detroit parts plant the management informed white workers that several Negro workers were to be upgraded from their foundry jobs into regular production work. The white workers replied they would not work with them if they were. The day before the transfers were to become effective, a white worker blacked his face with soot and another put him in a wheelbarrow and wheeled him through the plant, announcing, "This is what we're going to do with the niggers when they come in the department."

The next day two union representatives went to the plant and with management's permission called a meeting of the white employees. In effect this is what they said. "These Negro brothers are entitled to these jobs according to the seniority rules which you helped to establish. Your violation of those rules will weaken them much more than management's violations ever could. These men are going to have the full support of your union in asserting their right to work on the jobs to which they have been assigned. Anybody who doesn't want to work with them can quit."

The white employees went back to work. The Negroes took their places at their new jobs. Nobody quit. And there hasn't been any interruption in production since that time in that plant.

And Winn concludes:

The UAW–CIO's leadership is impressed with the importance of increasing our speed. They believe that labor has the answer to our race problem and that it can and will be solved through workers' realizing that division by race is a false and a weakening division that retards their economic and social advance. They do not believe it is an automatic process that moves inevitably and unswervingly toward a solution. They know that weakness on the part of local, state, and national officials can postpone and impede, if not block, a solution. They know that employers who refuse to accept their responsibilities can sabotage the program.

They know that another race riot can happen in Detroit, or somewhere else, and that it can spread to the plants, if it lasts long enough, and destroy everything the union has accomplished.

They know that within the ranks of the union, against the thousands of members who recognize the necessity for solidarity between the races, there are some Chrysler and Ford workers who still mutter, in private conversation, "Those black bastards tried to break our strike." They know that there are native Fascist groups and probably Axis agents whose business it is to keep alive this feeling.

They know that arriving at a solution requires courageous leadership on their part and resistance to any temptation to take a seemingly easier course. They are not *certain* of victory. But they are certain they have found the way to victory.

There is a welcome agreement on the cause and cure of the trouble between progressive union leaders and the younger spokesmen of the Negroes themselves. For example, Roi Ottley in *New World A-Coming* says in effect:

> Chronic unemployment was the major factor that set off the riot (of 1933). After long periods of enforced idleness, able-bodied men, unable to support their families by their own toil, turned to petty crime and vice. Because of the inability even to maintain themselves simply, many women turned to stealing and others to prostitution.
>
> Unrest in the adult population was reflected by the children. Deprived of home supervision or places for wholesome fun and facing a blind alley of opportunity, youngsters congregated on street corners where they witnessed the most sordid forms of crime. Many were either truant from school or would steal fruits from the stands of venders, drink whiskey in basement dives, and frequent dance halls, gin mills, and poolrooms.
>
> All this went on before a backdrop of greasy and rundown tenements in filthy and evil-smelling streets. . . .
>
> Essentially, the masses of Negroes are concerned only with jobs—for they believe that fundamentally their problem is an economic one. They want the "FOR WHITES ONLY" signs torn from every job in American life.
>
> The integration of Negroes in our economic life would end differences and divisions between the races now accentuated by their separation.

Another Negro, Earl Brown, in the Public Affairs Committee pamphlet, *The Story Behind a Race Riot,* comes to almost similar conclusions in explaining the more serious disaster of Detroit, June 21, 1943, where the war had accentuated the problems of housing the extra half million of various races who had shifted into the Detroit area in the period, June, 1940, to June, 1943. Mr. Brown, however, shows that in Detroit religious intolerance and anti-Semitism were also present. If you want to find historical precedent in the Protestant Church, you can look up the anti-Semitic declarations of Martin Luther. See, for example, the statement in *Behemoth* by Franz Neumann (p. 94).

The unspeakable and bloody persecution of the Jews in Europe by Hitler has given the Jewish problem a new and awful urgency and made the general public conscious of anti-Semitism in the practices of many American industrial groups. The details of such discrimination in industry, education, and the professions are too well known to this group to need citation here. Toward the end of his brilliant analysis of anti-Semitism as "the successful technique of counter-revolution" and the way in which it "sheds light on social pathology as a whole," David Riesman in "Politics of Persecution" (*Public Opinion Quarterly,* Spring, 1942) also focuses attention upon economic action:

> Action must be taken with reference to the roots of our social and economic difficulties. If these difficulties are straightened out by vigorous democratic action, we will have gone a long way towards arresting the tide of anti-Semitism and its complete eradication; if not, they will produce their desired fruit in Fascism. We could rest assured, for example, that when American society treats Negroes as equals it must have repaired those inequalities in which anti-Semitism flourished.

Such a view goes deeper than the dismissal of anti-Semitism given by George Bernard Shaw to the *Sunday Express* early this year:

> Anti-Semitism is the hatred of the lazy, ignorant, fat-headed Gentile for the pertinacious Jew who, schooled by adversity to use his brains to the utmost, outdoes him in business.

Harold J. Laski (*New Statesman and Nation,* Feb. 13, 1943), in noting the disturbing wartime growth of anti-Semitism in Britain and America, also put the Jewish problem in a larger setting:

> So long as the social and economic environment was favorable to democratic expansion, so long the preservation of Jewish rights seemed part of the faith of civilization. But psychologically, as it was the latest, so it was the weakest, part of that faith. It was always rooted in a soil where ancient memories made emancipation a tree of hesitant growth, fragile and

uncertain of its right to spread. Whenever democratic expansion halted, it was the first principle to be threatened with the axe. . . .

Yet the burden of our history is unmistakable; the enemy of the Jew is the enemy of freedom. They who organize the pogrom today will attack tomorrow the general foundations of freedom. That is why the moral stature of a nation is set by its recognition that the claim of the Jew to freedom is the claim of its own people to strike off its chains. When it is silent before the agony of the Jew, it collaborates in the organization of its own future servitude.

Unless countermeasures are taken, anti-Semitism will not end with Hitler because in postwar problems we face again the periods of social transition and maladjustments which have always in history used the Jewish people as a scapegoat. Anti-Semitism is likely to be again the barometer forecasting social storms.

This paper began with the global effects of ending group discrimination in industry as manifested in Jim Crow and anti-Semitic practices. The small and immediate things we must do on our own doorstep and at our work bench are the indispensable items which will add up to the desired result.

There can be no doubt that the nonaggressive type of Negro becomes less representative. Hortense Powdermaker in "Negro Aggression and the Cultural Process" (*Journal of Sociology,* May, 1943) notes "a decline in religious faith" as a factor because the younger people "are much more hurt by slights and minor insults than their parents because they do not put their faith in the promise of a heavenly victory." As the Princetonian alumnus, Andrew J. Hatcher, wrote to the students of his alma mater:

> If you discriminate against me because I am uncouth, I can become mannerly. If you ostracize me because I am unclean, I can cleanse myself. If you segregate me because I lack knowledge, I can become educated. But if you discriminate against me because of my color, I can do nothing. God gave me my color. I have no possible protection against race prejudice but to take refuge in cynicism, bitterness, and hatred.

Economic frustrations are a basic cause of group discrimination. Hence the trade-unions and business concerns are strategically on the spot and can do most to tackle the problem and secure a real equality. That is why the FEPC and its case against the Southern railroads and unions provides a real showdown. Indeed Winifred Raushenbush in the December *Survey* asserts that ". . . the fight to keep, strengthen, and make permanent the FEPC is the battlefront which will determine whether postwar America will be a democracy in anything except name."

It would be foolish to expect unions not to share the prejudices of the communities in which they operate or to expect them to forget so quickly the one-time role of the Negro as a scab and his use by business to cut down wages and extend working hours. Here education for the unions must supplement all legal compulsions.

Unless people get to know each other and seek to avoid offense, group defamation and group discrimination will continue despite laws to the contrary. And little things add up. A Negro girl of my acquaintance, Frances H. Williams, has written a short guide to behavior for whites:

> Try for one week to include every Negro you meet, as you go about your ordinary life, in the human family. Help him to feel like a man.
>
> (1) Say "Good morning" to the janitor, the Negro newsboy.
>
> (2) Try calling full-grown Negro men and women whom you don't know well, "Mr.," "Mrs." and "Miss." It's magic. Don't worry that others do not—just do it yourself.
>
> (3) Provoke good behavior from a tired, cross Negro. Even if he is in error, assume your share of the blame. Say casually, "Sorry, my fault."
>
> (4) In a shop meeting, help the silent Negro to participate in the discussion.

Included in her advice is "Work with a mixed group where the main problem is not racial, *e.g.*, a labor union." Frank Crosswaith and Alfred Baker Lewis in a *Social Action* pamphlet have also some excellent advice on what each of us can do. See also "There are Things to Do" by Lillian E. Smith, reprinted from *South Today*.

There are a thousand and one things we can do. Our own individual attitudes should be examined with care to prevent any foolish reference made in levity, injuring the feelings of any race. Negroes do not like the half-idiot, half-angel mammy of Hollywood. They do not like such analogies in public speech as "the nigger in the wood pile." They like to see the word *Negro* spelled with a capital initial letter. The least thing we can do is to avoid such mistakes, often made in ignorance.

There is little basis of fact in most of the stereotypes of various national groups and their alleged traits and behavior. The most generous people I have known personally have been Scotsmen and Jews. I have known many Irishmen who had no sense of humor. I am sure you have known stupid, ignorant Jews as well as brilliant intellectuals of that race. Upon close examination, not one of our stereotypes will stand up to the examination of people as people in the twentieth century.

The Durham, Atlanta, and Richmond statements made by bi-racial meetings of Southerners and published by the Commission on Interracial Co-operation; the work of the Council of Democracy in setting up the Negro Press Conference and in working out techniques for introducing Negroes into industrial plants; the agitation against the poll tax, against segregation in education, in the Army, in housing, in the Red Cross blood bank; the proposal to rewrite history books to give the Negro long overdue recognition and to remove offensive reference to racial minorities; the forthright declarations of the CIO against the Jim Crow and Anti-Semitism; the work of N.Y. State War Council's Committee on Discrimination and its success in aiding management to integrate Negroes in war industries as described in its pamphlet of that name; the action of the NLRB in treating discrimination in the case of the Boilermakers Union (Alameda, Cal.) as an unfair labor practice, thus supporting FEPC; the move to give FEPC itself full statutory powers equal to the NLRB of which it might become a part—all these are hopeful trends in the current pattern of activity in which we all must participate. For, make no mistake, if group discrimination persists, Hitler wins, and democracy is doomed.

BIBLIOGRAPHY

Neumann, Franz, *Behemoth,* Oxford Press, New York, 1943.

Northrup, Herbert R., *Organized Labor and the Negro,* Harper, New York, 1944.

Persitz, Milton, "Jews in Government Service," *Congress Weekly,* March 27, 1942.

Reich, Nathan, "Post War Economy and American Jewry," *Jewish Review,* May, 1943.

Weaver, George L. P., *Role of Organized Labor in Education for Racial Understanding,* 7 pp., Congress of Industrial Organizations, Washington, D.C.

Williams, Frances H., *Speak for Yourself,* mimeographed, author, 1612 S Street, N.W., Washington, D.C.

X

RELIGION AND MINORITY GROUPS

BY

BISHOP H. ST. GEORGE TUCKER, D.D.

I am very grateful for the privilege that has been accorded me to speak on this subject. I am also conscious of my lack of qualifications to discuss the subject.

I have had some experience with religious minority groups because for twenty-four years I was a member of a minority group out in Japan, consisting of 300,000 Christians as compared with the 60 millions of non-Christians. Therefore the question of minority religious groups in the midst of a tremendous majority of people who had a different religious attitude was a very real problem.

I think, first of all, it might be well to say just a word about groups, their functions, and the dangers that are involved in their formation. After all, the progress of civilization has been greatly expedited by the group-forming tendency of our human nature. People with a common interest, people with a common purpose organized themselves into a group, and it was only in these groups of individuals collaborating one with another that certain problems could be worked out. That, of course, is the value of the group system.

The danger of the group system seems to be this: that while the group serves a valuable purpose in that it enables the individual to transcend his own interest and devote himself to a cause which is a good deal larger than himself, yet the very loyalty which he comes to feel toward the purposes of the group often is accompanied by an equal indifference to the interests of those who lie outside of its borders. That would not make so much difference if that loyalty confined itself to the specific purpose of the group to which he belonged. But frequently the loyalty developed among members of a group not only becomes an effort to serve the purposes for which the group was originally formed, but extends into all the varied interests of mankind.

As we know, in the world of today, our greatest menace comes not so much from selfish individuals who are pursuing their own purposes as from certain groups who try not only to dominate the sphere in which they are particularly interested, but also to extend that dominance into all the various spheres of society.

If I may give an illustration drawn from the country in which I lived and from the sphere of religion: There was a time back in the sixteenth century when an effort was made to Christianize Japan. For a while that effort met with a great deal of success. There were probably more Christians in Japan in the sixteenth century than there were in the nineteenth century and yet that effort ended in complete failure.

While these Christian converts aroused a certain amount of religious antagonism on the part of the Buddhists in Japan, in the beginning they were regarded with a good deal of complacency and indifference by the authorities. These Christian missionaries gradually were so successful that they made converts of the chiefs of many of the feudal clans in a certain section of Japan. There were some thirteen or more feudal chieftains called Daimios by the Japanese who became Christian converts.

It happened in Japan at that time that some particular clan would be dominant in the country as a whole and the other clans were always striving to overthrow the dominance of the ruling clan. These Christian converts, being bound together by their common adherence to Christianity, became involved in politics. They were mostly in the southwestern part of Japan, and it is quite a distance from the place where the ruling clan had its headquarters. The ruling clan became suspicious that the combination of these Daimios would finally end in the overthrow of their own power in Japan, and as a result of that they began a very strenuous persecution of the Christians, largely on the ground that they were Christians.

It is interesting to note that, at that time, Hideyoshi, who practically dominated the whole country, didn't say that he was afraid that these Christian Daimios would overthrow the power in Japan.

The Buddhists, as you know, did not eat meat. They do not believe in killing. They have the Eastern idea of the transmigration of souls and that you ought not to kill any living thing.

Hideyoshi said: "These Christians are beef eaters and, therefore, they ought to be thrown out of the country." That is the excuse he gave for the persecution of Christians.

My point is that as long as the Christians had confined themselves to their own specific interests, that is, the Christian religion, the rulers in Japan were not particularly interested. They may have been Buddhists themselves, but there was no great religious antagonism on the part of the educated classes in Japan. But the moment they went out of their specific field and entered into the field of politics, there they aroused a tremendous antagonism.

So we modern missionaries who belonged again to a religious minority in Japan at least learned the lesson that if we were to be tolerated in that country we had to confine ourselves to our own sphere and that Christian converts, when it came to politics or any other question, must consider those questions on their merits and not act together as a unit so that you would have an organized minority acting together on any question that might arise.

I think the Japanese Government today would look upon Christians who acted in that way as just as much a peril to the national welfare as Hideyoshi considered the Christians in the sixteenth century.

Now if I may use another illustration: I happen to live down in the South. Of course, the problem of the Negroes is a great problem there. The Negroes constitute not a religious minority, but they do constitute a racial minority, as you know.

I remember some time ago receiving a letter from a clergyman in New York State. He told me he had spent the preceding winter in South Carolina and he was very much shocked at the way the South Carolina people treated the Negroes and he said, "I wish you would issue a public reprimand on the way they treated those Negroes."

I told him if he knew the South Carolinians as I did, he would know that would not be a safe thing to do.

I do not think there is a tremendous amount of race antagonism in the South. We have been living with the Negroes for quite a long time, but, unfortunately, after the Civil War, during what is called the Reconstruction Period, most of the white people of the South were disfranchised and the franchise was given to the Negroes.

When the Negro race became involved in politics, there was a rise in antagonism which was due to the fear that this racial minority might become a dominant power in all political matters.

There was a story about a former Confederate general who was quite a leader in the white group that used the Negro vote in order to establish its power. The story is that the general was going up to heaven and he met an old Negro coming back. The Negro said to him, "General, there is no use in your going up there. I have just been there. When I knocked on the door, they asked me if I was riding or walking, and when I said I was walking they wouldn't let me in."

The general said to the old Negro, "You get on your hands and knees and I will get on your back and ride up and we will both get in."

They went up to the gate and St. Peter said, "Who is there?"

"General Mahone of Virginia, sir."

"Are you riding or walking?"

The General answered, "Riding."

St. Peter said, "Just hitch your horse outside and come right in, General."

That is what really happened to the Negroes.

There again my point is that, as long as the Negroes constituted a racial minority and as long as their interests were devoted to the welfare of the racial minority, I do not think that anybody would have been unduly concerned. But the minute the Negro went into politics and, of course, it was right that he should go into politics, the minute all of his political attitudes were determined by a racial connection and he voted as a *bloc* in politics, then the people in the South became very much alarmed.

While that danger of dominance through the use of the Negroes has long gone by in the South, yet there are politicians who use that fear as a threat to compel all the white people to vote *en bloc* on the side which they think the Negro is not going to be on.

So that it seems to me that one real problem with a minority, whether it is a religious minority or a racial minority, is that, as long as you have a minority group in which men are bound together in their loyalty to some particular issue and as long as they confine themselves to that issue, then there is a fair chance that a minority will receive equitable treatment from the majority that lies around them.

But the moment the minority begins to extend its group loyalty and to work together and to act together in matters that are outside of its own specific interests, the minute you feel that you have a minority group in your midst that on whatever issue arises does not determine its attitude on the general merits of that issue and asks not, "What shall we do for the welfare of society," but determines its attitude from the point of view of its own minority interests, then antagonism against that minority will inevitably be aroused.

I know it happened in Japan, and it happened down in the South with the Negro. The right of minorities to their own views will be recognized as long as they confine themselves to their own special lines of interest, but this is not altogether true because majorities are just as arbitrary as minorities are. Majorities very often wish to use the minorities for their own purposes and, when they cannot use them for their own purposes, they become exasperated so far as the minority is concerned.

It seems to me that the greatest protection minorities have from ill-treatment from the majority is to act together in whatever matters are of common interest to them, but in matters that affect the general interest, their attitude should be determined by the welfare of society as a whole and not by the interests of their own group.

I know that during the years I lived in Japan we were let alone by the government, because the government felt we were not a menace to the general policies of the government.

On the other hand, as this war began to draw near, there was on the part of the militarists in Japan a very definite suspicion of the Christians, because they felt that somehow the Christians, because of their views, would be opposed to the nationalistic policies of Japan. Fortunately, that did not result in persecution. I do not know whether the Christians became just as great nationalists as the rest of the Japanese, but at least they did refrain from interference in political questions and thereby escaped a persecution which might have been just as violent as the persecution which took place in the sixteenth century.

I should like to stress just this one consideration: in so far as a group develops a group loyalty among its members wider than loyalty to their own personal interests it performs a very wonderful service to society. But just as soon as that group loyalty takes the form of loyalty to the group as an end in itself, and all human questions are determined from the point of view of the group, so that the world outside is looked upon simply as a field in which the group can operate in order to strengthen itself and promote its own interest without any concern for the welfare of society as a whole, at that point the group becomes a distinct menace, and if it is a minority group, it is likely to suffer pretty severe treatment on the part of mankind as a whole.

That is true of the Negroes in the South. I think it is because the political leaders of the South are able to persuade the white people that we have here a group that is always going to act together as a group, is going to consider every question from the point of view of the Negro and not of the Negro as an American—it is because of this that there is so much prejudice and antagonism to the Negro.

In speaking to Negroes, I always try to impress upon them that, if they wish to have justice shown them, if they wish to have a fair opportunity here in America, they must think of themselves first of all as Americans and secondly as Negroes. That doesn't mean that groups should be done away with. That doesn't mean that the racial distinction should be abolished, because the real problem we have in this world is not to reduce all men to a uniformity. That is the theory of certain people.

After all, we are striving in the world of today for two great purposes: one is what we call freedom, and the other is unity—world unity. To many minds freedom and unity are incompatible terms, because just so far as individuals are free they will develop diversities, and in the minds of a great many people diversities do not tend toward unity.

We believers in religion, we who believe that God has made of one blood all nations of men, believe also that in our own common relationship to the one divine Father there is the possibility of combining diversities into a real unity. The races are different, the nations are different, but in our religion we feel that there is a principle which is able to take things that are diverse and bind them together into a real unity without abolishing the differences.

It seems to me that the minority groups perform great services. In the first place, they do help to preserve that diversity without which the human society would be monotonous and uninteresting, and yet at the same time a minority group, if it does really believe in God who has made of one blood all nations of men, can find a principle of unity which enables it to co-operate with other groups in promoting the welfare of society as a whole.

That seems to me to be the point of view that religious minorities should hold very clearly in mind. Each religious minority has a contribution to make. It adds to the diversity of human society. It probably has seized upon some point of view that has been neglected by others and, if it can maintain that point of difference up to the point where it is a contribution to the richness of the whole, if its members do not become fanatics and feel that their own point of view must be imposed upon everyone else, if they do not arouse a fear among other people that in every question that arises they are going to act together as a minority group and try to make a minority into a majority which dominates and destroys all other points of view, then it seems the minority has a fair claim to consideration and perhaps will receive justice from the majority group among whom its members reside.

Our own country affords a splendid opportunity for the application of this principle. There is no country in the world where there is more variety than here in America. We are made up of men of all races, we are people who because of our loyalty to the idea of freedom have developed a tremendous amount of diversity. We are divided into a number of states, each one of which has a certain amount of local self-government.

We have an opportunity to show to the world that it is possible, through our loyalty to something which transcends all the differences of groups existing here in America, to combine those groups together into a real whole. That is the problem that confronts the world today.

I have been very much interested in this. I was over in the Far East some four or five years ago and I traveled around a good deal and met a great many people. I thought it was rather pathetic how everyone was looking over to America to see if America did not have some message of hope; whether there was not some gleam of light coming out of America which perhaps would afford an answer to the problems that were oppressing and bearing down on idealists in that part of the world.

And yet one wonders whether that is true. America today is like that city which we were told is set on a hill and the nations of the world are standing around watching us to see whether this system of freedom, which creates diversity and yet which we claim is able to combine that diversity into a real unity, whether that is going to work, whether it is possible to do that in a country like America. If we are able to solve that problem here, if we can take our groups as we find them and, without destroying the groups and group differences, combine them together into loyalty to a common cause, to a cause which is as wide as humanity itself, then it seems to me we will have made a contribution of inestimable value to the problems confronting the world at the present time, the problem of combining all the races, all the nations, all the religions of the world into one common group which might justly be called the Family of God here upon earth.

XI

RELIGION AND GROUP TENSIONS

BY

REV. JOHN LA FARGE, S.J.
Editor, "America"

Religion has been greatly interrogated of late as what it can do for the peace of the world. But the matter of group tensions is at the heart of most of the questions of peace; and religion's work for the unification of mankind is at the heart of much of this particular problem.

Many years ago, when some of the elder members of this audience were small boys, there were serious group tensions on West Fifty-third Street and vicinity in New York City. The tensions manifested themselves in the form of brickbats thrown by Irish youth at the heads of juvenile Negroes and returned with interest by the recipients. After a time some wise men among the Negroes concluded that the tensions had about had their day and that it would be advisable to abolish them. This was clearly a job that required statesmanship; so they took counsel with New York's most prominent statesman at that period, the Hon. Charles F. Murphy, boss of Tammany Hall. Mr. Murphy agreed with them as to the futility of such tensions, enjoined Tammany's followers to call off tension-inspired activities, and peace, a durable peace, then descended upon West Fifty-third Street and San Juan Hill, with the concomitant and consoling result that now, for the first time in Manhattan's history, Negroes were becoming a recognized and important sector in the Democratic as well as the Republican party.

Statesmanship, too, can solve many a problem of tensions in our day, whether they be between national groups—in the interests of world peace; or between domestic groups, in the interests of civic harmony. But statesmanship is encountering some rather rough going in the international field, and it can do much, but not everything, in the field at home. Religion's voice is hard to raise amid the roaring and thumping of those who insist that the majority that has the power is the majority to be obeyed. The New York *Daily News* or the Washington *Times-Herald* makes more noise than the identical seven-point Declarations of the religious leaders issued on October 7 of last year. Nevertheless, religion's voice is not silenced, when the din lulls; it is heard announcing the same eternal and unchanging truths, and that voice reminds us that statesmanship can go so far, but no farther: there comes a point where force, even when exerted in the highest interests, defeats its own end. The final arbiter in group tensions, as in all other human affairs, is man's conscience, and it is to conscience that religion directly and authoritatively speaks.

To review all the angles with which religion conveys a message on group relationships would be, of course, a treatise on social ethics. It would mean that we should review religion's teachings on the dignity of the human person, his natural rights and their bearing on the security of the individual. It would mean, also, that we would recall another phase of religion's teachings, which is the broad question of human unity, the natural unity of the human race. All these matters are familiar to you and have doubtless been dwelt upon by previous speakers in this course.

I shall confine myself simply to one of these many angles, which opens up, I think, a certain very practical and timely perspective.

When we talk about group tensions at the present moment, we are really concerned about two different things, which are at the root of these tensions. These things are similar and closely related, but they are not identical, and one may have one of them without the other. The first set of phenomena concerns various forms of intergroup *prejudice,* all the ways in which we fear, distrust, and dislike people of other social groups, whether these be national or racial, cultural or religious, and so on.

Religion's teachings warn us against the objection, very obvious and frequently made, that religious people are often found among those who most readily yield to prejudice. The answer may be made that religion is an intensely vital thing, but, like all vital things, it must be taken in its entirety. It cannot be assimilated merely in any one part of our being; it must penetrate the whole; and, therefore, where this phenomenon is found, it is not due to a lack of vitality in religion itself, but to its imperfect assimilation, its faulty application.

The other set of phenomena goes way beyond the realm of mere prejudice and enters into the field of myth. The myth is a positive, concrete, historical thing, in contrast to the merely subjective phenomenon which we entitle prejudice, even though that subjective phenomenon, or state of mind, may be embodied in custom, law, or institutions.

The myth is a movement; it is a rationalization, not merely of this or that local situation, but claims to be an interpretation of history. It explains why the world is as we find it, who are the ultimate sinners, what is the great threatening danger that lurks behind all the passing scene, and it has the character of a mystical absolute.

In his recent monumental work, published by the Carnegie Foundation, the Swedish sociologist, Gustav Myrdal, ably analyzes the function of the social-equality myth with regard to the Negro in the South. He shows how, once that particular idea is admitted as an inevitable law of his being—that the Negro must somehow always be seeking social equality, that is, intermarriage with white people—everything else follows from that, everything is seen from that peculiar perspective.

We can catalog a whole series of myths of the same kind—the idea, for instance, that the Catholic Church is necessarily seeking political power; that the Jewish people are eternal conspirators against the established order of things and are seeking to dominate the world; that Great Britain's propaganda is omnipotent, and is most effective when it is most invisible, and so on.

My point is not to discuss the myths, but merely to point out that they form a distinct factor in group tensions. They are an enlargement, a projection on history, a projection into the whole mystical and spiritual field, of some small and vulgar stereotype.

The myth, however, grows, attains its maturity and enrolls its followers in a religious vacuum. In this respect a singular phenomenon sometimes escapes our observation. It is this: that the teaching of religion with regard to the human family has a mysterious and powerful opposition to the predominance of these antisocial myths. Let me give a single instance. The most concerted and most elaborate and intelligent attack we have upon the institution of the family in our day is that of the Nazis. Those who know Hitler and his system appear to be emphatic in their pronouncement that he has a peculiar antipathy to the family as such. The whole course of his ideology is anti-family—to break up the home, to destroy the respect of the young for their parents, and to create a completely different concept of the fundamental unity of society. Some of the statements that have been made by religious leaders in neighborhoods that have been disturbed by racial strife have called attention already to the intimate connections that exist between these propaganda movements and the integrity of the family. The matter so far has only just been touched upon, but I believe European experience will deeply confirm this analysis and show us that it is a matter to be pursued much more carefully and thoroughly.

Religion, however, works not merely by its teaching but also as an institution, as a religious community.

The tendency in the modern world to look upon religion simply as an individual experience has caused us to overlook the important social function of the religious community as such.

Here again we observe a powerful force tending to overcome group tensions. As compared with the past, in some ways religious community suffers a certain eclipse. The traditional form of religious community is largely patterned according to the agricultural community, or at least a community of small and closed areas where there are more or less natural boundaries. It has been difficult for the religious community in any of the religious groups to adjust itself to the rapid transportation and mobility and the economic penetration of modern life. The difficulties are grave, as all pastors of souls will acknowledge. Nevertheless, I believe that these difficulties are only temporary. But like everything else in the history of religion, they can be overcome and will be overcome in the future.

A religious community has in the past derived a strength and stability and an absence of group tensions from common economic occupations or the close economic interrelations of its members, in the older type of community. In the future these more or less natural associations will be replaced by more deliberately sought voluntary groupings, such as locational grouping, co-operative organizations, and various joint enterprises. But when this equilibrium is restored it will be a powerful agent in bringing the full force of religion to bear upon the serious group conflicts. We need not look to the far distant future for that. I believe that in innumerable neighborhoods precisely the same operation can be set on foot at the present time.

I have in mind, for instance, the experience of a Catholic parish in Brooklyn with which I am well acquainted where there have been serious interracial tensions owing to migrants and the change of neighborhood in the residential area. The clergy in that particular parish found that the development of an interracial consumer co-operative turned out to be a method of bringing about racial harmony in a very difficult situation. Much more than any exhortations or formal instruction, the common working together of their parishioners of different races in a joint enterprise not only enabled them to know one another better but it also enhanced their mutual self-respect; it brought out the best in each race and has been a powerful factor in stabilizing that particular area.

In conclusion, let me say that religion works not only by its teaching, not only by its organization or institution, but it works also by the regeneration of the individual. Here we come to the supreme test of the power of religion in the modern world. All the teaching, all the organization will be in vain unless the individual is consecrated in his own personal life, unless he develops within himself that inner spring of spiritual energy and of selfless charity which will enable him to take upon his own person the burden of the social conflict. Here again we see that what was looked upon as a vexing and annoying circumstance is developing into a wide field of spiritual opportunity. It is, to use the hallowed phrase, a means of sanctification for the individual. Since God our Father has called us to sanctification we are foolish, each one of us, not to make ample use of the means that are at hand. I believe that we shall see a great development in individual regeneration, as we will in religious community organization, in the not-far-distant future. Let us thank the good Lord, Who has brought all social groups together, that He has given us this greater opportunity to advance His Kingdom.

XII

DEMOCRACY AND MINORITY GROUPS

BY

DONALD R. YOUNG, PH.D.

Professor of Sociology, University of Pennsylvania

World War II is accepted by the mass of citizens of this country as a war of survival between democratic and Fascist governments. The Four Freedoms, the Atlantic Charter, the Teheran Conference and a constant stream of official statements by all the United Nations emphasize the necessity for victory if democracy is to survive. *Mein Kampf,* edicts, laws, and actions of the Axis powers make plain the undemocratic plans of the enemy. The people of this nation believe that they are fighting for the very existence of democracy.

Ideals, however, are not often put wholly into practice even by groups who would fight and die in their cause. An outstanding example of such conflict between ideals and behavior is the undemocratic discrimination against minority peoples of divergent racial or recent alien origin so widespread in democratic America. The present war with its democratic slogans and the need of total military and civilian mobilization has sharpened the consciousness of all minority peoples and of many of the dominant majority concerning this paradoxical situation. It has perhaps been most forcefully expressed by those Negroes who campaigned not just under the V for Victory slogan, but under the Double V banner, one V for victory on the battle fronts, and a second V for democratic victory at home.

"Democracy," however, is a word which means many things to many people. To the lawyer it is likely to mean conformity to the Constitution of the United States in accordance with existing laws and court decisions. Present purposes, however, do not require that we accept the lawyer's concept, for we are not trying to plead a case in court. We are seeking to gain understanding of a problem of human relations, and problems of human relations are better understood through the application of scientific knowledge and ordinary common sense than through the examination of legalistic writings. We are all deeply attached to the principles of democracy, but most of us have only the foggiest notions about them when forced to put our thoughts into words. Possibly the one idea we all have about democracy as it is popularly understood in this country is that it implies a live-and-let-live mode of existence, with respect and freedom of opportunity for the individual in so far as consonant with the general welfare in present circumstances. This is a vague and unsatisfactory statement when one attempts to apply it to specific troublesome situations, but, because it is about what people mean when they talk about democracy, it is the only satisfactory point of departure for a discussion of democracy and minority groups in our society.

Popular concepts must also be used in defining minority groups. Social scientists and others interested in race relations have too commonly made the error of assuming that they have logically settled the matter when they have proved in a scholarly manner that there is no such thing as a pure race in the United States, that observable inborn racial traits have not been shown to have any necessary relation to ability or character, that such words as Jew, Italian, Nordic, Aryan, Russian, etc., are biologically meaningless, or that psychological tests have failed to demonstrate group inferiority or superiority. All we can actually show by such evidence and argument is the falsity of a current rationalization of discrimination against minority peoples, a useful but inconclusive achievement. Group discriminations do not originate in nor depend upon theories about any unalterable hierarchy of races. They are social phenomena, and the objects of discrimination are necessarily socially defined.

In other words, a person belongs to a minority group if the people of the community believe that he does. A person is a Negro if he is so regarded where he lives. The same may be said of an Indian, a Jew, or an American. This does not mean that minority individuals may not, as groups, have differentiating biological and cultural characteristics. Indeed, possession of some distinguishing marks is necessary for the ready identification or what has been called "social visibility" of group members. Actually, however, specific individuals belonging to minority groups may not have any of the characteristics attributed to the group as a whole, and most members may lack one or more of the alleged group characteristics. Proof of essential identity of a person of minority status with one or more members of the dominant majority is relatively unimportant in either study or argument about group relations. What counts is what people believe, and why they believe it.

The problem which we face, then, is that of reconciling the popular belief in democratic principles in the United States, on the one hand, with prevailing beliefs and practices concerning minority groups, on the other. This problem is not a new one; it embroiled the early settlers of the country and has troubled each succeeding generation. Now, however, its identification with the world-wide struggle makes a solution more urgent and strengthens our desire to effect one. We could, of course, reconcile conflicting ideals and practices by modifying our ideals in an undemocratic direction. With this remedy the present author has no concern except one of fear that it may be accepted by default of those whose social values should motivate an active crusade against it.

Campaigns by those who believe in a fundamental revision of undemocratic practices, rather than of the American creed, have utilized many methods, and we may well review some of the most common.

There is first the exhortatory attack, which has its roots in our religious heritage. This line of approach assumes that people can be made to see the light by strong urging, earnest advice, and warning. This may have been an effective means of persuasion in earlier times, but I suspect our changing culture has reduced its value as an instrument in reform. Many people today have been trained to be skeptical of sermons, lectures, and tracts. The present emphasis is on scientific knowledge and practical programs based on facts. Tests of social attitudes have been given experimentally to audiences before and after exposure to exhortation, and the results support the view that this sort of attack has relatively minor effects. People are still easily led but in our present culture too few will be led by reformist exhortation to place much dependence on this line of attack. There is a further disadvantage in its use by the protagonist of more democratic practices: it can always be used by his adversaries and perhaps with greater success, since they are all too likely to be unhampered by the ethical standards which democratic peoples respect and try to follow. In Germany the Nazis made the most of this advantage.

Some method more compatible with our modern civilization seems to be in order. The high value placed on facts is an outstanding characteristic of this civilization. We have come to rely on their power and on that of science and of education to accomplish any desired ends. It is only natural that we should appeal to facts in a campaign against discrimination. The facts of natural and social science, in my opinion, justify the conclusion that the interests of the dominant majority in this country will be best served if discrimination against minority groups is eliminated. It seems very doubtful, however, that the widest publication of all the relevant data in appropriate media of communication would end discrimination against minorities in this country, although the influence would certainly be felt. Even if the facts were placed in the hands of the people whose practices we would change, we could not be sure of the result. The same set of facts can lead to different and sometimes exactly opposite conclusions by different persons because of subjective factors affecting their judgments. Social attitudes are seldom the product of logical reasoning, nor are they most readily altered by logical argument. Fundamentally important and popular as it is, something more powerful than the appeal to facts is needed.

Some have sought the solution in legislation and the courts and still have great confidence in this approach. But only rarely and in a small proportion of cases can discrimination be prevented by appealing to the law or legal agencies. Residential segregation is not a matter of law. Exclusion from restaurants, failure to obtain service in commercial establishments, inequalities in the administration of justice, restriction in employment and recreation, and other types of discrimination cannot be corrected in the courts except in a relatively few instances. Of course, specific individual injustices can be corrected and damages awarded in cases of injuries to individuals in certain circumstances, but this approach does not promise a general solution of the problem.

How much the legal attack on discrimination should be intensified and expanded is a question. The importance of appeals to law in individual instances of injustice should certainly continue to be stressed. So far as the need for new laws is concerned, there are numerous statutes on civil rights applicable to minorities now; the difficulty is that they are not enforced. There is need of an organized effort to promote their enforcement, for, in addition to righting wrongs to individuals, the law has other important functions in the fight against discrimination. Statutes may make explicit the gains already made, and they may state the official position of the nation on the issue of discrimination as a goal toward which to strive. Enforcement of two types of law is involved: first, the general laws which should be enforced equally for all regardless of majority or minority status and, second, the special laws which guarantee civil rights to minorities specifically for their protection. Enforcement of the first type is by far the more important since the mere fact that there is need for enactment of the second is evidence of the essential weakness and relative unenforceability of the first. This is itself a reflection of popular feeling and indicates the extent of our failure to solve minority problems by this method.

What, then, of the efforts of the minority groups themselves? Direct action has been shown to be a powerful method of attack. Minorities can do much to improve their condition by exerting economic and political pressure, if they have the advantage of possessing something which the dominant majority wants. In times of labor shortage the range of occupations open to members of minority groups can be extended and their working conditions can be improved. Campaigns based on the slogan, "Don't buy where you can't work," have brought results. The scramble for the Negro, the Polish, the Jewish, the German, the Irish vote, and the votes of other groups in the history of this country and in recent elections shows what can be accomplished politically if it is to the interest of a majority group. The minority which possesses a political balance of power in any area is in a very strong position. The danger in the use of this or any other form of pressure is that the development of minority solidarity may be carried to a point where lines of cleavage become too sharp and intergroup tensions threaten to break out in conflicts which may cost more than the immediate gains.

Much has been made of the possibilities of united action by several minority groups, but the advocates of this theoretically powerful use of pressure are probably doomed to disappointment. American history does not reveal many instances of successful collaboration on a large scale by several oppressed minorities. In this country some of the larger groups can easily distinguish a common goal, but they are not likely to unite effectively in a joint campaign to attain it, because their own prejudices militate against any such procedure. And for this they do not deserve censure; we may hardly expect minority peoples to exhibit qualities of leadership, co-operation, and forbearance superior to those characterizing the larger population of which they are a part. It is unreasonable to ask them to demonstrate extraordinary abilities even in their own defense. It is, furthermore, probably overoptimistic to assume that any appreciable number of the dominant majority can be persuaded to exert active pressures to abolish discrimination. The motivation is not often strong enough in the face of the many interests competing for attention today. The attack by group pressures will probably remain a responsibility of the separate minorities themselves.

All these methods of attack on the problem of conflict between our democratic ideals and the actual treatment of minorities—exhortation, education, legal action, pressure tactics—work to some extent, but none is as effective as its advocates might hope. This is because discrimination against minorities in the United States is not so simple that it can be explained in terms of evil intent, ignorance, legal failure, ineffective use of pressure potentials, or any other single factor. It is all of these, and more.

Strategically, this means that there is no simple way to abolish discriminatory practices. If those who want to see intergroup conflict and unfair treatment eliminated do not want to be cast in the role of distressed and wishful thinkers, they must make an effort first to understand why the situation exists and then employ every practical device to weaken and destroy its causes. Discrimination exists in this country because an indefinite but appreciable proportion of the people want it to exist. They want it because they have been taught to dislike or fear groups of people whose looks or behavior differ from their own. The fear may have its roots in economic or some other form of competition. Its origin may have been forgotten. But through tradition and early training the members of the dominant majority have learned that discrimination is a way to protect themselves from the competition and threats, however fancied, of the minority groups. Thus discrimination is an accepted American way of responding to certain situations, while it is at the same time contrary to American ideals of democracy, to the personal ideals and standards of behavior of large numbers of Americans, and to the best interests of the nation in peace or in war.

To change this pattern of behavior we must first decrease the fears which have perpetuated it. Specifically, reduce the threat of economic competition and whatever other threats, real or imaginary, are known to worry members of the majority or to be used by them in rationalizing their attitudes or behavior. A practical program to reduce the social visibility of our minorities would reverse Hitler's measures to increase anti-Semitism in Germany. He increased awareness of the Jews and assured their identification by marking their clothing and their places of business, by designating special areas where they could live. He increased fear of the Jews by a constant stream of propaganda emphasizing their success and their wealth, asserting that they monopolized the professions, ran the government, held all the best jobs, and so threatened the welfare of all the rest of the population. His campaign was very effective in Germany and in a good part of Europe; its influence reached across the ocean to this country.

We can find other clues as to how to decrease visibility and fear of minorities by examining the course of discrimination against particular groups in the United States. Some of the immigrant groups, the Irish for example, were formerly considered undesirable, but, although their descendants are relatively numerous, they are no longer considered a group apart. They are not easily identified; the once distinguishing features of culture, accent, or costume are gone. Some prejudices remain, but they are relatively unimportant. Similar observations can be made concerning the Germans, Scandinavians, and later immigrants from Southern Europe. In the case of these groups which are not sharply differentiated by outstanding inborn racial features, discrimination fades as assimilation erases visibility, unless something is done to interfere with the process and to keep awareness of differences alive.

Another factor which dispels fear is small numbers. Even in the case of a racial minority easily distinguished by physical characteristics, discrimination disappears when the group is small, unless there is too great concentration in one locality. The American Indian, once so feared that he was likely to be killed with slight excuse, is now thought of as the noble vanishing red man. The racial features of the Indians have not changed; they are still visible but they are not feared because their numbers are now so small in proportion to the total population. However, in those regions where Indians are concentrated there is still some prejudice and some discrimination. We see the same phenomenon in the historical shifting of attitudes toward the Oriental immigrant groups on the West coast.

In the single case of the Negro, both numbers and visibility are such that awareness and fear are less easily decreased. But fear can be reduced by seeing to it that white people become familiar with the fact that Negroes can do and are doing everything that anyone else does. A campaign to make Negro activities of all kinds usual and matter-of-fact will both allay fears and reduce social visibility in spite of great numbers and biological visibility. *But* such a campaign must emphasize differences neither by stressing alleged special abilities and accomplishments, even though they are considered to be of high social value, such as dancing, musical, or dramatic talent, nor by needlessly overemphasizing mistreatment and conflict. The former unconsciously lends support to theories of race differences. The latter sharpens issues, increases visibility and fears, and can do little more than increase general awareness that there is a "Negro problem." We have too great a tendency, in our efforts to prove that there is no basis for discrimination, to stress the exceptional qualities and achievements of all minority groups instead of concentrating on making their participation in all the ordinary aspects of life so commonplace that it does not cause concern. The current campaign against anti-Semitism is wise in that it does not accentuate special Jewish contributions to modern civilization, does not needlessly publicize cases of discrimination, and does as little as possible to bring Jews to the attention of the nation as Jews.

In the efforts that have been made to improve race relations, perhaps the greatest strategic mistake has been that of confusing goals with programs. How often have the anti-discrimination books that we have read, the lectures we have heard, and the discussions in which we have participated, merely elaborated the goal and proved that it was desirable without telling how to reach it? Americans claim to be practical but their approach to problems of race relations has been analogous to saying, "There ought to be a law." With any other goal, which is as clearly apprehended, we know that a practical program is necessary for its achievement, whether it is to make a million dollars or to be president! But when we are concerned with group relationships, we have a tendency to state our goal and then become irritated with those who ask for details about how to reach it. We may even call them names, such as opportunists, compromisers, Tories, Fascists, or worse, if they are satisfied to move slowly or will for the time being accept anything less than the total goal. The Nazis and the Fascists made no such mistakes. They had a racial goal for a purpose and they knew what had to be done to achieve it. It is incredible that we should help them do it simply because we can only state that the integration of democratic principles and intergroup behavior is our goal and vow to hold to it, when we should be actually blazing the trail by work on a planned program of practical accomplishments.

BIBLIOGRAPHY

Young, Donald R., *American Minority Peoples,* Harper, New York, 1932.

Young, Donald R., *Minority Peoples in the Depression,* New York Social Science Research Council, 1937.

Young, Donald R., "The American Negro" (Editor), *The Annals of the American Academy of Political and Social Science,* Vol. CXL, Philadelphia, Pa., November, 1928.

Young, Donald R., "Minority Peoples in a Nation at War," *The Annals of the American Academy of Political and Social Science,* Vol. CXXIII, September, 1942.

XIII

THE ORDERING OF A MULTIGROUP SOCIETY

BY

R. M. MacIVER

In the course we are concluding, we have viewed from many different angles what is a major source of discord and unease in the society in which we live. The unity of the nation, the strength and well-being of the community are being threatened by the maladjustments and the frustrations that arise in the relations of group to group, by the prejudices and suspicions and the hostilities and the fears and the discriminations that arise between group and group. It has become, I believe, perhaps the major problem of our particular society at this particular time.

The issue is not the difference between groups, but the way in which we react to these differences. The issue is not the conflict between groups. Everywhere men and groups are engaged in some kind of struggle. Everywhere men and groups are, among other things, seeking to get ahead, and, while it has its harmful effects, it also has its beneficial effects. In any case, it is the condition of a dynamical society, and it is not here our concern.

We are concerned in this course with something different, with something more sinister. We are concerned with the disabilities, whether for co-operation or for competition, that exist between group and group, with the exclusions, with the denials, the rejections that keep groups apart, that shut groups up so that they do not share in the common fresh air of the world in which we live, with exclusions and denials that threaten their personalities, that obviously interfere with their life chances everywhere, that invade their integrity, that poison the springs of life and of faith.

Here has lain the concern of our course, in those relations between group and group and in those denials and exclusions and discriminations that are contrary to the fundamental principles on which this country is presumed to have been founded. This source of discord and unease has not been growing less in our day; it has been growing greater.

We have seen in the various talks given in this course that the threat to our society from this source is a real and a grave one. We have seen that it permeates every sector of our social life, that it enters into our economic relations, into our social intercourse, into labor organizations, into professional organizations, into every aspect of life. In every relation of life it tends to frustrate, to thwart the hopes and disturb the innermost thoughts of groups. That is why I dare claim that it is perhaps the major problem of this present society at this present time.

I do not propose to review the various statements that have been made by the different speakers in this course. They said many illuminating things, and they gave us wise counsel, but these things are in the record, and I shall not seek, in the time I have, to cover that ground again. I should, rather, prefer to go back of the things said. In the light of what has been said in this course I should like to review the whole issue, and especially the question of how to attack it—the question of how we can in some degree remedy this situation, remove so far as we can this great and growing trouble.

In a peculiar sense, this issue of group relations is a problem of our own country. In this country we have reached the ground for a higher stage of civilization with respect to groups and their relations, because in this country we no longer identify the people or the state with any ethnic group, with any faith, with any section, and therefore, for us in this country it is not a problem for political reform, as it may be in the first instance in many parts of Europe.

We have passed that stage on the whole. If we lived up to our Constitution and our codes, the difficulties we are suffering from would largely disappear. There may be some changes we should make in this respect but, on the whole, we have already conquered the political citadel. The trouble is that constitutions and codes do not control men's thoughts and actions and attitudes.

With us the trouble is not mainly one of political relations. It is not one, in the first instance, of the guarantee of civil liberties by constitutional law. It is a question of our social relations, it is a question of our social attitudes, and the reason why our codes and our Constitution in this respect are not too effective is that there is a discrepancy, a disharmony between the legal, the political side, which we have won, and the social side which we have certainly not yet won.

So the main issue is that of a better ordering of group relations. The question is for us one of our response to other groups, of our attitudes toward other men, and that should be the controlling fact in any program we offer, in any steps we take toward betterment. The controlling fact is the need for social education, for social re-education. What can we do about it? If I am right in saying that the essential trouble—while there may be things that can be corrected here and there by changes in provisions and regulations—lies in social attitudes, then there is no short or easy road to our goal.

In fact there is a danger in taking short cuts to this goal. We must not only have our hearts in the right place, we need wisdom as well as right emotion if we are going to face this question; and our emotion, unless it is guided by wisdom, will make things worse instead of better. Sometimes that has happened among us.

The trouble does not lie with any particular group. The trouble lies between groups. It is the question of the relations between them, and therefore, to remedy it, we cannot seek a specific for a particular group alone. We probably should not concentrate too exclusively on any one group when it comes to the matter of saying what should be done to improve things.

We cannot get ahead far by pressing the particular claims or the particular rights of any one group, because so long as you are doing that, first, you are not touching this matter of social attitudes, and, second, you are still putting the accent on difference, and that is where a large part of the trouble lies. Instead of finding remedies for this group, for the evils, the troubles, the discriminations that this group or that group suffers, our main task is to advance along the whole front. Otherwise, we may gain a little here, but we lose it because we do not hold the line. The line has not gone forward, and the line is the line of our social re-education.

This statement may be misunderstood. I do not mean to suggest that we should not take steps to expose the discriminations that particular groups suffer from. I do not mean to suggest that we should not be active in showing up the evils of discrimination in particular instances and its effects on particular groups. What I mean is that, having done so, we must proceed to apply a larger principle that is relevant to all groups. What we do for one, we are doing for all, we are doing for ourselves. The accent must not be on difference, because that is already our trouble.

The ailment does not depend on the existence of any particular group, no matter how manifest the trouble may be with respect to it. The evil is a universal one. Sometimes it is one group, sometimes another. Sometimes it is, say, the radical; sometimes it is the liberal. Sometimes it is the Roman Catholic, sometimes it is the Jew, sometimes it is the Protestant. It depends on the conditions where the evil strikes. But its root is the same always, without reference to the particular people who may be the particular victims at any one time.

Therefore I do not believe we are going to get very far in solving this problem merely by strong advocacy of the claims of any one group, or by showing—good as the case may be—the contributions that any one group makes. That is all very well in its place, but it is not the solution of this problem. You may recall that in one of our discussions there was some difference of opinion on this point, as to whether it was a good thing or not to have, let us say, a Czech hour on the radio, a Greek hour, or an Italian hour, and so on. I tended to side with those who thought that it had little efficacy for this particular purpose.

It is like this: You have an hour on the radio, let us say, or a column in the paper. How does it look to the outsider? The rest of the time the radio is American, and this hour is Czech. That is what it looks like. In other words, you are separating the group from the totality of the community.

On that occasion I suggested that we might even claim that to have a "woman's page" in a paper was itself an invidious and possibly odious affair, if you really saw it right, unless you had also a "man's page." All the rest of the paper is for the dominant majority, and we will give one page to the women! But that point raises a question I would rather not discuss!

What we have to advance toward is the common rights of all groups, and we can help by showing how some are denied these common rights, and proceeding to indicate these rights in the name of all rather than in the name of any group.

All groups everywhere are different. All men everywhere are different. So there is no question in any sane mind of an attempt to abolish differences. It is not even a question of the assimilation of differences, if you mean by that expression the reducing of them to one uniformity. Nor is it a question of the toleration of difference. To be tolerant is still like giving some group their hour on the radio. You give them a little space; after all, you allow them to exist. But tolerance in the long run, though there are times when it is a necessary first step, is really an insult. It is not tolerance that is the issue. It is the reception of the differences into the unity of the whole society. And that is quite a different thing.

These differences, I say, exist everywhere, and the trouble is that we misconceive them all the time, misconceive what they are and misconceive what they mean. We do so because it is around differences that our group egoisms and our group interests cluster, and so the assertion of difference is associated with claims of superiority, denials of equality; and differences tend to be distorted into the caricatures that our prejudices and our ignorances create.

Such distorted ideas of other groups abound where, as peculiarly in these United States, we have a multigroup society. They do two things that are contrary to truth. First, they exaggerate the difference between the group that makes them and the group they are supposed to represent. They give the one group many virtues, and, of course, they give the other group many less favorable qualities. Thus they exaggerate the differences between groups, and, even more, they exaggerate the likenesses within the single group. They suggest quite fallaciously that those who belong to a particular group are extremely alike in certain important qualities.

All groups do this thing. Minority groups do it as much as majority groups. Subject groups do it as much as dominant groups. We all do it. We paint unflattering pictures of other groups, and we come to think that every group is a rather simple embodiment of a particular set of attributes. For example, you find the Gentile's conception of the Jew uniform, as if there were one kind of human being called a Jew and he was like that everywhere. Whereas actually, if any comparison is possible here, Jewish people are one of the most variant of peoples, not only if you think in terms of differences of origin, but if you think of differences of individuals, families, and subgroups. Nevertheless, the Gentile still cherishes the simple image of the Jew. Of course, if they knew how they quarreled among themselves, perhaps they would change their minds!

All groups are always doing that kind of thing, perverting our relations because we meet in terms of these pictures and not of realities. I suppose we do it partly because it is easier. It is a lazy substitute for understanding, but, even more, we do it because it is the best support for our group pride, our group interests, our group prejudices, whatever they may be. These emotions are sustained by nothing so much as by our carrying around in our heads these unfavorable images of groups that are not ours.

So it comes back to this: that the major task, if we are going to get ahead, is the task of social education. What do we mean by that? What can we do by that? There is a great fundamental premise that somehow we have to get across in education. The premise is that what we have in common is more fundamental than what we have separately, that that which unites us is deeper, more profound, more important, more real, than that which separates us.

It is very necessary that this fundamental premise should be stated and restated with all the ingenuity we can display, and it is particularly important in this day and age because we live in a time when every group is organized, when every group has its special voice, when we have new devices of propaganda for spreading these voices. Since everybody belongs to a group, these group voices fill the air. We hear these warring voices all the time, but we do not hear the voice of the whole, the voice of the community, and we have to find some way of bringing that common voice to the hearing of the people.

Education can be set going in many ways to this end. I am not suggesting that there are not other important steps. I am merely saying that the fundamental way to form a better-ordered society is the way of education, because the great trouble lies in our attitudes. Our first job is to show up the falsifications that come from the tensions between group and group. We have to show how these bring danger to the commonweal, to our own country, and beyond that to our common humanity.

We can start in the schools. At present we have practically no *social* education. We educate people in civics and so forth, but that is really secondary. If you educate people socially you educate them concerning the way in which they should be related to other men. That is primary. We can start with the schools, and if we get it in the schools, we shall get it in the families, we shall get at the springs of indoctrination.

We must enlist, also, the churches, the various faiths, and if we succeed here we can go further and have an impact on the more distant chambers of government.

I suggest that this is the order in which to proceed: to proceed from the family, the people, and the church to the state, and not the other way around, in this educational program.

It is a vast program, a very difficult program, you may think. True, but at the same time there are many agencies that can be enlisted if we set about it. It is a good sign, as Doctor Finkelstein has mentioned today, that this need for social education is beginning to be realized. We are seeing signs that the churches are to a greater extent becoming aware of the need. Our friend, Doctor F. Ernest Johnson, is helping in that respect, and there are a great many others who are helping, too, but it is only a beginning—a much greater awareness is needed.

Before we go much further in that awareness, we have to set down certain lines upon which this teaching can develop. To begin with, there are two sides to the teaching itself. We have to expose false teaching, we have to show the consequences of that false teaching, because they mean a serious disruption of the whole basis of our common life. Then we have to help spread truer views about men and groups and the relations between them, truer views of the nature of society, truer views of what civilization means and how groups belong together within this civilization, truer views about this American society of ours, which peculiarly depends for its strength and stability on the spread of these truer views.

There are two media through which such instruction can be conveyed. One is the living word, the great medium of the word. The other is our way of life. One without the other may be vain. In other words, we have to give examples, we have to *live* relationships. Examples spread, both pernicious ones and the others, and if we combine the word with a way of life that represents a truer sense of relationship between groups, then we shall get ahead.

I believe the time has come for a really great social movement in this direction. Our generation has been going through a time of war and upheaval and crisis and tension. That period has been a bad one for the harmonious relations between men everywhere, not only between countries but within countries. All have been affected by this atmosphere. Even those who fight in the name of democracy against intolerance may become affected somewhat by the very thing they are fighting against. There is a danger because the evil is in the air, and it is congenial to a time of war and tension.

We need to bring that time to an end. There is great need of new goals and new standards. Of course, nothing would help it so much as if we had a peace of understanding between peoples and an end of the stimulation of hatreds between peoples, because that spirit penetrates down into the smallest group.

It is very largely a question of bringing men to see what perils our society is facing. In this day we have to get beyond the narrow group ethics that tend to dominate us, the narrow group ethics which, when we have no great binding faith, separate group from group. Each group has its own purposes, and it struggles for these purposes. So we have the ethics of the group but we haven't the ethics of the whole. We have to get beyond the fragmentation ethics of a divided society.

That is the trouble of our time. We have to appeal to the more universal, to the common. It is there if we take hold of it. The great faiths, although they speak with different voices, have all back of them a certain universality of ethics that is entirely opposed to this fragmentary ethics of the divided group. We have to appeal there, and in the last resort we have to appeal to the understanding and the hearts of men. We have to think in terms of new standards and new goals, and we should think of a charter, a sort of charter of human relations that needs to be set up. Our age needs a new, a somewhat different charter, a charter that will think not of the relations of individuals, but of the relations of groups, so that groups may be unified freely without loss, without prejudice, within the whole.

That unity is so much deeper than the differences that, once people see it, they cannot lose it any more. To teach this lesson is the great task of social education in the strictest sense of that word. Through social education alone can we attain this salvation of the society in which we live. To teach it we need new modes of expression, new forms, new words, new symbols.

As you have gone out of this building, you have noticed that over the portal there is a symbol, the symbol of the burning bush, the bush that burned but was not consumed. I have more than once reflected on coming inside this door that I, too, in a far-off island, was brought up in a church which had that same symbol, a different church. It suggests something, that the symbol is greater than our differences, and we need symbols for this unity. That symbol of the bush that burned, the tree that was not consumed, suggests the kind of living spirit that animates, endures, lights, warms, but does not destroy. We can think of that as the spirit of man, the thing that has to be rescued from these differences. We can think of that tree as the symbol, and we may, perhaps, add to it another saying about a tree whose leaves were for the healing of the nations.

INDEX